# Emerging Challenges to Mission

# Emerging Challenges to Mission

EDITED BY

Siga Arles

2012

**Emerging Challenges to Mission** – Published by the Rev. Dr. Ashish Amos of the Indian Society for Promoting Christian Knowledge (ISPCK), Post Box 1585, 1654 Madarsa Road, Kashmere Gate, Delhi-110006.

© ISPCK, 2012

---

*All rights reserved. No part of this book may be reproduced or transmitted in any form or by any means, electronic, mechanical, photocopying, recording, or by any information storage and retrieval system, without the prior permission in writing from the publisher.*

*The views expressed in the book are those of the contributors and the publisher takes no responsibility for any of the statements.*

---

ISBN: 978-81-8465-262-8

*Laser typeset by*
**ISPCK,** Post Box 1585, 1654, Madarsa Road, Kashmere Gate, Delhi-110006.
Tel: 23866322/23
e-mail: *ashish@ispck.org.in* • *ella@ispck.org.in*
website: *www.ispck.org.in*

# Contents

Foreword
   – *Ashish Amos* ... vii

Introduction
   – *Siga Arles* ... xi

Challenges of Contextual Mission Today
   – *Felix Wilfred*     1

Rethinking the Mission Paradigm in the Light of Emerging Challenges: A Critique of the Missional Church
   – *Kieran Beville*     15

Rhythm of God's Heartbeat: Biblical Perspectives on Mission Theology
   – *Kieran Beville*     38

Reading the Bible for Inclusive Justice
   – *Monica Melanchthon*     63

## Contents

Role of Churches in Nation-Building
    – *Roger Gaikwad*      76

Promotion of Social and Economic Equality in India
by the Church as Participation in Mission of God
    – *Sunil Michael Caleb*      88

Indigenous Dalit and Tribal Missiologies and Missiologists
    – *Siga Arles*      101

Urban Mission In India: Transformational Engagement
    – *Richard Howell*      125

Feminist Perspectives in Mission
    – *Bernadette O Connell Beville*      148

Mission Engagement with Entertainment:
Place of Christian Story in Fiction and Film
    – *Davis Bunn*      159

Preaching Christ in a Postmodern Culture:
From Congregations to Audiences
    – *Kieran Beville*      168

**The Way Forward ...**      ...      **182**

**Contributors**      ...      **185**

**List of Participants**      ...      **188**

# Foreword

The book, *Emerging Challenges to Mission*, is an informative compendium of some of the quality papers presented at the Mission conference organised by Indian Society for Promoting Christian Knowledge (ISPCK), Delhi, as part of its tercentenary celebrations held in October 2010.

It may be mentioned that more than forty-five ecumenical scholars, including theologians, missiologists and Episcopal leaders, convened for consultation on the theme, "Mission Priorities and Challenges: 2010 and Beyond", and all of them gave valuable insights into the process of Mission in India and abroad. Virtually all of them agreed that missional efforts need to be 'inclusive' and that the church in India should not be an 'exclusive' church. This explains why this book has been titled "Emerging Challenges to Mission."

Certainly, Prof. Dr. Siga Arles has displayed admirable perspicacity in choosing the papers for this volume, as all the papers presented at the conference bear the mark of clarity of thought, scholarship and theological acumen.

The opening chapter of the book is aptly titled "Challenges of Contextual Mission Today", as it focuses on the need for a new praxis of Mission. According to Prof. Dr. Felix Wilfred, the social, political and cultural situation in India presents enormous challenges to "Christian mission praxis" and to be able to respond to them, we need to "reflect theologically in context." After presenting five sets of fundamental challenges to today's mission, he concludes the paper by pointing out that Mission can take place without "foregrounding the Christian identity" and that Mission implies learning, overcoming the teaching complex and creating inclusive communities.

In the next chapter, Dr. Kieran Beville focuses on the need for rethinking the Mission paradigm in the light of emerging challenges. His paper is an insightful critique of the Missional church. According to Dr. Beville, the church is an organism, not an organisation; it is a "living, dynamic and organic entity of the redeemed" and evangelism is not an elective element of the spiritual life.

In the chapter that follows, Dr. Beville focuses on what he calls "rhythm of God's heartbeat" and presents biblical perspectives on Mission Theology. He says that our theoretical presuppositions about Mission and our theological rationale for Mission need to be determined by the Word of God; the Scripture should be allowed to speak for itself as the missionary manual; and "understanding the rhythm of God's heartbeat is about being in tune with his heart and being in touch with what he is doing in contemporary culture. Being missional minded is about seeing as God sees..."

In the chapter entitled "Reading the Bible for Inclusive Justice", Dr. Monica Melanchthon maintains that we need to pay heed to the voices of the marginalised, for in doing so "we participate in and continue God's work of redemption and reconciliation." She believes that those who follow Jesus Christ must work for the liberation and transformation of structures and systems and that "incorporating the realities and struggles of the marginalised majority is a theological and missiological imperative..."

The next chapter focuses on the role of churches in nation-building. Rev. Dr. Roger Gaekwad points out that around fifty years ago, the church contributed a lot towards nation-building through educational institutions, medical services, technological training centres, orphanages, old people's homes, facilities for the blind, houses for juvenile delinquents and so on and that the church should continue with such ministries by "ensuring high standards of service without commercialising those ministries." According to Dr. Roger Gaekwad, the church should also advocate for alternative economies, technologies and ways of life.

In the first section of the next chapter, which is entitled "Promotion of Social and Economic Equality in India by the Church as Participation in Mission of God", Rev. Dr. Sunil M. Caleb establishes the extent of inequality—social and economic—in today's India. In the next section, he shows that inequality is against the will of God because it "complicates the building of community." He then goes on to focus on how we should participate in the mission of God, which is "to struggle against the forces that perpetuate inequality."

In the chapter entitled "Indigenous Dalit and Tribal Missiologies and Missiologists", Prof. Dr. Siga Arles identifies Missiology as a subject, locates the study of Missiology within Indian theological education, enlists the scholars that emerged as missiologists from among tribal Christians and Dalit Christians, discusses the indigenous quality of the kind of Missiology developed by these missiologists and considers the way forward in developing indigenous Missiology from Dalit and Tribal scholars.

In the next chapter, which is entitled, "Urban Mission In India—Transformational Engagement", Rev. Dr. Richard Howell maintains that the process of urbanisation presents innumerable challenges for urban Mission. Christians living in cities must therefore be informed and equipped to engage effectively in ministry and mission to the urban population. "Mere sociological analysis", to put it in his words, "will not suffice; the city has to be skilled in exegesis as well."

Bernadette O Connell Beville says that God has given His gifts to the church without a gender bias and without a bias of race or location. In her paper entitled, "Feminist Perspectives in Mission", she says that men and women are one in Christ and that there is no distinction between the two. According to her, since the rise of women's liberation in the 1960s, there has been a discernable development of a feminist critical consciousness in secular society and in the church. She says an evangelical egalitarian model, which sees male and female as created equally by God in Genesis, has become a reality. However, "the evidence of poverty in women's lives", to put it in her words, "and their ongoing abuse in sex trafficking is deeply distressing and has to be addressed."

Davis Bunn feels that there is a strong need for Mission engagement with entertainment, as we live in an entertainment-driven world. In his paper entitled, "Mission Engagement with Entertainment: Place of Christian Story in Fiction and Film", he says that India's middle class is not just growing, but becoming a dominant force, and so Indian evangelists should try to involve themselves in the lives of this growing component of Indian society; it is necessary for them to engage with the middle class on its level, with a clear eye to its interests. Davis says that "story may provide the perfect conduit."

In the closing chapter, which is entitled, "Preaching Christ in a Postmodern Culture: From Congregations to Audiences", Dr. Kieran Beville avers that preaching Christ is feasible in postmodern culture. According to him, the church needs to understand the historical and philosophical development of postmodernism; it must recognise that the Enlightenment project has lost its influence and that Christianity is perceived as nothing more than a meta-narrative. He feels that some guidelines about preaching to postmoderns are needed and that the notion of persuasion needs to be redefined as "a whole-soul influence affecting the mind, emotions and the will."

I strongly feel that the valuable insights given by the scholars at the Mission conference would give new directions to the process of Mission in India. Needless to say, these insights have helped ISPCK in drawing up its agenda for the fulfillment of its Mission in future.

**Rev. Dr. Ashish Amos**
General Secretary
ISPCK, Delhi

# Introduction

Indian Society for Promoting Christian Knowledge (ISPCK), Delhi, celebrated its tercentenary in style at Cathedral Church of the Redemption, New Delhi, with the Archbishop of Canterbury Rowan Williams as the chief guest and a number of bishops and leaders of the various churches and organisations of India as honoured guests. After the thanksgiving service with elaborate liturgy and eucharist in which the Archbishop rendered a brief homily, we were entertained by the cultural performances given by students at various schools of Delhi. It is indeed noteworthy to register the history of the efforts made to spread Christian knowledge through literature by the faithful team of missionaries and other Christians in Delhi and elsewhere in the country—wherever ISPCK has its branches.

The next two days, that is, 16-17 October 2010, drew a group of more than forty-five ecumenical scholars—theologians, missiologists and Episcopal leaders—from various church denominations to ISPCK Mission Conference to focus on the theme: "Mission Priorities and Challenges: 2010 and Beyond."

The challenges of today's contextual mission were identified by the noted Catholic scholar, Felix Wilfred. He identified five sets of fundamental challenges in binary form: (1) Incarnation and Prophecy, (2) Service and Radical Transformation, (3) Identity and Crossing of Borders, (4) Teaching and Learning and (5) Compassion and Inclusive Communities. He lamented "the absence of a vision for the world, for society and for the well-being of humankind and nature" and called for "a renewed praxis" to meet "the new challenges and frontiers of mission" in India. According to him, "Today we need to build up inclusive communities. This is the ultimate guarantee for the practice of human dignity and rights. Creation of inclusive communities applies both for the Church as well as for the society."

An Irish mission thinker, Kieran Beville, reflected "rethinking on the mission paradigms in the light of emerging challenges" and enlisted "biblical perspectives for mission theology" to keep "mission at the centre of church life" and shared his concern from his context of "preaching Christ in a postmodern culture." Monica Melanchthon offered fresh insight into inclusive biblical interpretation to avoid the process of exclusion in mission. Roger Gaikwad saw the mission of inclusion from the angle of "the Church's role in nation-building", while Sunil Michael Caleb specifically saw mission as "the promotion of social and economic equality in India." Richard Howell summed up the contours of "urban Mission in India", while Bernadette Beville reflected on the "feminist perspectives in Mission." Siga Arles explained the development of Missiology as a discipline in India, elaborating especially on the growth of mission thought, theology and commitment among the indigenous peoples—the tribals and the dalits. Davis Bunn drew our attention to the need for Christian mission to penetrate the contemporary world through the skillful use of fiction and film and raised issues for Indian Christians to consider and urged them to develop a creative future for Missional communication to the masses.

Interestingly, various authors interpreted the process of Mission as having changed from exclusion to inclusion: There is a need for presenting the gospel and living it in such a way that people do not feel excluded by our Missional efforts but are drawn to Christ through our imitation of him! It is not an isolated and separatist church that we aim to build but a community of humanity that is redeemed, healed, liberated, made equal and dignified. This was the main theme of the conference. Hence the title "Emerging Challenges to Mission" for this collection of papers.

The scholars who participated in the conference moderated the sessions and facilitated meaningful, high-quality interactions. The purpose of the conference was explained by Rev. Dr. Ashish Amos, General Secretary, ISPCK, in his welcome address—to set an agenda for the kind of mission literature and mission themes that should be explored in fulfilling the mission of ISPCK in future.

I appreciate the hard work of Rev. Dr. Ashish Amos, Mrs. Ella Sonawane and Mr. Sandeep Chawdhry in organising such a high-quality Mission consultation. I was privileged to have edited and developed this volume, which I hope would be of much use in shaping our future mission thought and agenda in India. ISPCK should organise similar conferences in other parts of the country as well to give a fillip to relevant thought and theology to arouse the Church in mission for our times.

**Prof. Dr. Siga Arles**
Director
Centre for Contemporary Christianity,
Bangalore
April 2012

Chapter 1

# Challenges of Contextual Mission Today

## Felix Wilfred

Mission is *contextual*. It is invariably situated in a definite historical point of time and at the conjunction of different political, social and cultural forces. The changing times and contexts call for a continuous rethinking of what mission is and how it needs to be pursued. I am not entering into details regarding the change of understanding in mission;[1] rather I am focusing on the need for a new praxis of mission. The social, political and cultural situation in India and Asia at large presents unprecedented challenges to our Christian mission praxis. To be able to respond to them, we need to reflect theologically in context.

---

[1] For this, one may refer to the comprehensive work of David Bosch, *Transforming Mission-Paradigm Shifts in Theology of Mission*, Orbis Books, New York, 1997; see also Philip L. Wickeri (ed), *The People of God among All God's Peoples: Frontiers in Christian Mission,* Christian Conference of Asia & The council for World Mission, Hong Kong, 2000; see Felix Wilfred, "Our Neighbours and Our Christian Mission: Deconstructing Mission without Destroying the Gospel" *Ibid.,* pp. 78-100.

I want to present five sets of fundamental challenges to mission today—each one of them in binary form.

## I. Incarnation and Prophecy

To believe in incarnation is to put an end to all kinds of pernicious dualisms. God becomes in Jesus a secular reality (*saeculum*—the world) through a process of identification. "And the Word became flesh and dwelt among us." (John 1:14). It is this that has given room to speak of Christianity at the root of de-sacralisation and secularisation. A genuine understanding of incarnation helps us also transcend the model of two histories—one, history of salvation and the other, the history of the world.[2] There is but one single history in which our faith leads us to see the presence and working of God.

Incarnation has also a truly universal or catholic dimension. It embraces all human beings without barriers and accepts them in their context with their unique characteristics. Think of the Christian tradition of translating God's Word. It is God's Word *also in translation* because no language, no people are alien to the mystery of God who identifies herself with the people.[3] Translation is in a way a submission to what is not one's own. It is leaving behind one's familiar world and entering into a new world. We understand this point better when we take into account the fact that in Islam, God's Word is believed to come to humanity in the Arabic language, a status no other language can claim. The faith in God's Word that comes to us in our flesh, in our language, has contributed to valorise the cultures and languages of people, acknowledge and affirm them. The efforts towards what is known as inculturation or contextualisation in worship, art, architecture, theology, etc., are the reflections of the spirit of divine incarnation.

---

[2] Cf. Felix Wilfred, "A Matter of Theological Education—Some Critical Reflections on the Suitability of 'Salvation History' as a Theological Model for India", Vidyajyoti Journal of Theological Reflection, 48 (1984) 538-556.

[3] Cf. Lamin Sanneh, Translating the Message: The Missionary Impact on Culture, Orbis Books, New York, 2009; ID., Whose Religion is Christianity?, Wm. B. Eerdmans Publishing Co. Cambridge, 2003; see also William A. Graham, Beyond the Written Word, Cambridge University Press, Cambridge, 1987.

"For God so loved the world that he gave his only Son" (John 3:16). If that is the case, then the Church needs to love the world, society, cultures and traditions of people. This will be the witness to the incarnation. Incarnation calls for commitment to and active participation in the history of society, of the people with whom Christians share their lives. There is no end or limit to identification.

The question is: To what extent is the Church one with the people? What we note is the temptation of the Church to withdraw into its shell of security. The way of being Church with lack of identification lends easily to stigmatize it as *"foreign."* There is a lot of preoccupation with itself. Much time, energy and resources that should be spent on outward movement is consumed by internal questions and issues. The Church feels comfortable doing many things but not being with others. It runs *parallel structures* and undertakes isolated modes of activities and is self-satisfied. Christian communities and institutions take pride on their success. But when it comes to doing *with* others, there is reluctance and even resistance. There is no readiness to take the risk of doing with others, even if things do not go very "successfully."

In sum, Christian community is in mission when it lives the mystery of incarnation. Mission is promotion of God's incarnation today. Incarnation is not a single event of the past; it is a way of being and acting. There is then room to speak of "continuous incarnation."

Mission as incarnation and identification needs to go hand in hand with *mission as prophecy*. To be prophetic is a way of being and acting that is unconventional and most often unsettling. The prophetic nature of the mission of the Church tells us that it cannot get absorbed into what exists. The Church serves most effectively when it imagines and projects alternatives. Never satisfied with what is, prophecy is imbued with a sense of a future, more bright, more just and different. As the great Jewish biblical scholar Rabbi Heschel said, the prophets are those who sing one octave high.[4] By pointing to higher ideals and noble values, they make us raise our heads and look up. Powers that be, on the contrary, cover

---

[4] Abraham Joshua Heschel, *The Prophets*, Harper Permanent Modern Classics, New York. 2001.

up the truth and push it under the carpet to pursue a realpolitik and reap the advantages thereof. Prophets do not hide the truth but let it be seen by everyone. They are courageous to say that the emperor is naked.

Now one may be courageous but what he or she says may fall on deaf ears if that person is not rooted in the soil, incarnate among the people. We could discern in the Gospels two types of prophets, one in John the Baptist and the other in Jesus of Nazareth. John the Baptist was a prophet who was known for his austerity. In fact, he was brought up in the desert away from the people (Luke 1:80). People listened to him and his words forecasting the disaster that was to befall them. But the rest of the time, he was away from them and they did not have to worry much about what he said. On the other hand, Jesus of Nazareth, as the Gospels portray, was constantly amidst people. The Gospel says repeatedly that he was on his way, that he was everywhere surrounded by the people, so much so that Zachaeus had to climb up the sycamore tree to see him (Luke 19:1-10), and the paralytic had to be lowered through the roof to reach him (Mark 2:4). He was so much one with the people that they even accused him of being "a glutton and a drunkard" (Matt. 11:19; Luke 7:34). Precisely because he was one with the people sharing their life, he could also challenge them with his prophetic stance on various issues and with his radical teachings.

The mission of the Church, to be effective, needs to be really *rooted* in the soil and find itself where people are. In other words, the praxis of incarnation is the condition for effective prophecy. Viewed in this way, the challenges of incarnation and prophecy are not opposed to each other. They are two sides of the same coin. The point could be illustrated by the question of *caste* in Indian Christian history. When the Church was not identified with the people and rooted in their culture and tradition, giving the impression of a foreign body, its prophetic denunciation of caste failed to have any cutting edge. It was viewed as a critique from without. As it is, today, there is a failure on both counts— incarnation and prophecy. The challenge of mission then is for the Church to get ever closer to the people and at the same time never cease to be prophetic.

## II. Service and Radical Transformation

The involvement of churches in education, healthcare, upliftment of the poor, development, etc., have led many of our countrymen and countrywomen to see Christianity as synonymous with service. Obviously, service is the characteristic of a Christian inspired by faith and the teachings of Jesus. But service also needs to be placed in context. We need to think whether it turns out to be the kind of witness we imagine it to be. In a caste-ridden society, we cannot assume that service is perceived as witnessing, selflessness, etc. In reality, in a stratified casteist society, with clearly marked roles, service has been associated with the condition of the *shudra*. The Church in the subconscious of our countrymen and countrywomen is the collective *shudra* of society. It is viewed as the duty of Christians to serve, like it is the duty of the *kshatrya* to fight, and is taken for granted. After all, when Christians do works of service, they are just doing their duty, which they are supposed to do any way.

The many works of service churches do, thus, fail to make a dent, unless, the Church brings to the consciousness of the nation and in every strata of society, the importance of service that is incumbent on everyone and not only on the Shudra and the Church. It calls for a radical transformation both in the values of society and in the mindset of the people. "The Son of man came not to be served but to serve" (Matt. 20:28; Mark 10:45). This is the spirit of mission for every human being. There is the responsibility of every one for one's neighbour and for the promotion of common good. The casteist society with its watertight social compartmentalisation seems to pose today the question of Cain: "Am I my brother's keeper?" (Gen. 4:9).

So, what is required of the Church is not simply to expand its services—to build more educational institutions, hospitals and development works. The real challenge is to *universalise the spirit and motivation of service* behind these works. Serving others is not something exclusive to Christians. The spirit and practice of service is necessary for everyone to become a genuine human being. It is a force of life and it generates a centrifugal movement towards the other, in contrast to the self-seeking centripetal movement. Service becomes a concrete expression of the solidarity towards the other and responsibility to the well-being of the community.

The Church has immense opportunity to universalise the spirit of service. There are, for example, innumerable social activities in which the Church is involved. It runs about 400 colleges and 25,000 schools, where lakhs of children and students from different backgrounds and religious affiliation pass through. To what extent do these institutions instill the spirit of service in the minds of the young? When out of these institutions into their jobs or careers, many of them are found to be self-seeking, corrupt and casteist. Is this then not a time to think of the mission of the Church to contribute to a radical change in the way of thinking, behaviour patterns and practices? Here is a mission in depth. The mission, in short, is for a radical transformation of consciousness in the nation, among peoples and in every strata of society. It is a mission of every day for the disciples of Jesus.

## III. Identity and Crossing of Borders

One of the burning global issues of today is that of identity.[5] It is also a crucial question in present-day India. Identity is also an issue of major concern among religious traditions. The way we define Christian identity has a lot of implications for the praxis of mission. Can we understand Christian identity in such a way that it also defines what our mission is. Christian identity needs to be defined *in relationship* and not in isolation.[6]

Finding themselves in a minority situation, Christians and churches are prone to the temptation of fortifying their group identity. But we need to remember that Christians, like any other citizens in this country, have *multiple identities*. The relationship we forge on everyday basis reflects the plurality of our identities. In the context of communalism and violence, our religious identity as Christians needs to be viewed as an *open-identity*. This creates the right environment for mission, which will

---

[5] Amartya Sen, *Identity and Violence: The Illusion of Destiny,* W. W. Norton & Company, New York, 2007.

[6] Cf. Felix Wilfred, "Becoming Christian Interreligiously" in *Concilium* 2011/2, pp. 59 – 67.

consist of forging relationships with society, with cultures, with other religious traditions, etc. Open-identity leads us to dialogue with other religious traditions, with the social and political order, with civil society, etc. It is in this process of dialogue that churches will discern and discover the concrete mission in context.

In sum, *the challenge of mission is to cross borders*. But we may be inhibited to do this because of *tradition*. But then we need to critically view our tradition. Jesus did not say "I am the tradition." He said "I am the truth."[7] Mission needs to be centred on truth rather than on tradition. To the extent tradition serves truth, it acquires value and not *ipso facto*. Jesus did his mission by constantly crossing the borders—the border of purity and pollution, of ethnic identities, of religious identities, of social conventions like in the case of his dealings with women and women disciples.

To put it in theological terms, Christians are in mission when they follow the path of historical Jesus in mission. One cannot reduce this to a mission preaching about Jesus. His was a mission for the welfare and holistic salvation of all, that is to say, for the coming of the Reign of God. It coincides with the renewal of humankind and the entire creation. This mission, which is large and wide in scope, was the mission of Jesus, and it would find vibration among the people today. On the other hand, if we interpret mission as transmission of some truths embodied in our faith and belief, we may have to be disappointed. This was unfortunately the experience of many well-intentioned and dedicated missionaries whose preaching could not find much resonance among the people. Let me cite the case of L'Abbé J. A. Dubois (1765-1848) of French Foreign Mission Society. After over 30 years of mission work, he returned to his native France, a very disappointed man. This was due to the fact that he felt that there was no proper response from the people to the noble Christian truths he taught. Many of them relapsed and went back to their traditional religious practices, and those who remained, he found them to be the worst of the lot! His Three Letters on the State of Christianity had the subtitle "The Conversion of Hindoos [sic]

---

[7] This is what the early Christian writer Tertullian expressed when he stated: *Dominus noster Christus veritatem se, non consuetudinem cognominavit. De Virg. Vel.* 1, 1.

Considered Impracticable."[8] The case of Abbé Dubois may be a dramatic one. We can have some understanding for him taking into account the times he lived. Today, to continue to imagine that mission is transmission of Christian truths is to repeat a method that history has proved again and again not suited to our neighbours. To put it differently, speaking about Jesus of faith without Jesus of history in our mission praxis could alienate us from our neighbours. It is the praxis of the Church in the footsteps of Jesus of history that makes the Christian mission and witness credible and tangible today.

## IV. Teaching and Learning

"Go into the entire world and preach the gospel to the whole creation" (Mark 16:15)—this is the great mission command. A mixing up of the spiritual mission enjoined by Jesus with the ambition of political power—from the time of Constantine to the colonial history of recent times—has cost the effectiveness of the Good News. This has caused a sense of *alienation* among a large number of people in our own country. Let me quote from the celebrated book of K. M. Panikkar, a renowned historian and former Ambassador of India to China.

> It may indeed be said that the most serious, persistent and planned effort of European nations in the nineteenth century was their missionary activities in India and China, where a large-scale attempt was made to effect a mental and spiritual conquest as supplementing the political authority already enjoyed by Europe. Though the results were disappointing in the extreme from the missionary point of view, this assault on the spiritual foundations of Asian countries has had far-reaching consequences in the religious and social organization of the peoples.[9]

The teaching of Christian truths of faith by the traditional mission took place with a sense of religious and spiritual *superiority*, not to say arrogance. The others were viewed as objects for imparting knowledge and devoid of any light. The *teaching complex* of Christianity led not only to the neglect

---

[8] Abbé J. A. Dubois, *Three Letters on the State of Christianity in India; in which the conversion of Hindus is considered as impracticable*, Asian Educational Services, New Delhi, 1995.

[9] K. M. Panikkar, *Asia and Western Dominance*, George Allen & Unwin, London, 1954.

but to the denigration of the religious and cultural traditions of the people of this country. These were viewed as darkness to which the Gospel preaching was brought as the light. The focus was one-sidedly on the truth and its value that Christianity taught. It was not understandable for many missionaries—even today for many local evangelizers—how one could refuse to accept and adhere to the truth of Christianity once it is preached to them. This kind of claim by the self-proclaimed teachers of truth betrays two important things: First, the fact that those to whom Gospel is preached are *subjects*. They have their own history, world-view, values, choices, etc., all of which need to be respected. Second, it fails to focus on the welfare of the people, the nation or the group to whom the Gospel is preached.

Without attention to the subjecthood of the people and their welfare, the mission command turns out to be an aggressive proselytisation intended to strengthen Christian religious institution. Far too long the preoccupation has been on the message. The urge to communicate it was so overwhelming that in the process the well-being of the people to whom the disciples were sent was forgotten. There can be no teaching, no mission without attending to the welfare of the people to whom it is addressed.

The well-known Indian biblical scholar, George Soares-Prabhu, studied from a comparative perspective the great mission command in the Gospel of Matthew, with a similar command of Buddha to his disciples as found in the *Mahavakya*.[10] Reading the Matthean mission command in the light of the Buddhist command, he notes how in the Buddhist command, when the disciples are sent, the purpose of this sending is indicated, and indeed it is the well-being and happiness of the people to whom the message is preached.

> Go now, O Bhikkus, and wander for the profit of many, for the happiness of many and out of compassion for the world, for the good profit, and happiness of gods and human beings.[11]

---

[10] Cf. George M. Soares-Prabhu, "Two Mission Commands: An Interpretation of Matthew 28:16 -20 in the light of a Buddhist Text", in *Biblical Interpretation* 2 (1994, pp. 264-282).

[11] As quoted in George M. Soares-Prabhu, *art.cit.*

Added to the well-being of the people, the addressee of mission, the Buddhist command also speaks of the state of deliverance of those who bear the message. In other words, it speaks of the witnessing by the preacher. This is important for the credibility of the message transmitted.

> The Lord said to the Bhikkus: I am delivered, O Bhikkus from all fetters human and divine. You, O Bhikkus, are also delivered from all fetters, human and divine.[12]

Mission today is not only teaching but also learning, not only sowing but also reaping—yes, reaping the fruits of what God had planted in the minds, in the lives, in the tradition and cultures of our people. To be able to see this point, mission needs to be imbued with a *sense of mystery*. Mission preaching and teaching do not exhaust the mystery that is far beyond what we have come to know and experience.

True learning implies a *sense of wonder, amazement*. The Church needs to be taken hold of by what God has done in the world, in society, in cultures and religious traditions, without its instrumentality. The Church is not only called to be the mystery of God's love for the world but also to marvel at the wonders God has effected in the world. The more it marvels, the more it will be open to learn from the world.

Some Christians may argue: Why should the Church learn from the world, when it (Church) itself is the repository of God's revelation? There are many reasons for this learning.

First, from a theological point of view, creation is also the revelation of God; it is God's manifestation. All those wonderful realities the human spirit has created reveal also the divine mystery. As it is said, the first book of God is creation. To be able to understand it, God gave another book, the Bible. Second, as history shows, the reforms affected in the secular world often preceded the ones in the Church. The Church was reluctant, for example, to admit democracy, human rights, equality of women, religious freedom, ecological movements, etc. They first blossomed in the world, and belatedly the Church took them up as its own agenda. The developments in the world, if the Church is docile and

---

[12] Quoted *Ibid.*

ready to learn, could help it understand better the spirit of the Gospel and the path of Jesus. Third, the Church has no solution to all the problems assailing humankind. It is also groping and searching. It is also on a journey, as a pilgrim church. It needs to then take seriously many others on its way as its companions. Finally, the response to many questions and issues of today requires solidarity and co-operation among different moral forces. The Church needs to forge close relationships with them, particularly the various movements—the feminist movement, the ecological movement, the peace movement, etc. It is better to work with others even if everything is not perfect than doing everything perfectly all by ourselves.

## V. Compassion and Inclusive Communities

Like the problem of identities, *exclusion* is an issue that confronts humanity today. All over the world, we observe the practice of exclusion of different kinds, and they are present in our country and all around in our society.[13] There is a social hierarchy and religiously inspired hierarchies. "Homo hierarchicus" is how Louis Dumont characterised the caste system in the country.[14] Caste is not only a social structure but also a package of values and mode of behaviour. Hierarchy tends to be exclusive and it places people on a scale of high and low. Most exclusion is felt by the so-called outcastes, the Dalits. Patriarchy is also a form of hierarchy that subjugates women and places them in an inferior position to men. The challenge today is to move from all those practices, modes of thought and ways of behaviour that are based on inequality to the creation of inclusive communities.

Compassion is one of the important means by which the Church has been responding to exclusion. Mission work was accompanied by works of charity and compassion. Dedicated and heroic missionaries moved by compassion worked for the well-being of those living on the margins of society. Mission went to the periphery to remove the suffering

---

[13] Cf. Felix Wilfred, *Asian Public Theology*, ISPCK, Delhi, 2010.

[14] Louis Dumont, *Homo Hierarchicus: The Caste System and Its Implications*, University Of Chicago Press, Chicago, 1981.

of the oppressed, the victims. Today, compassion is not enough. The victims are not objects but *subjects*, with their own yearnings, dreams and aspirations. The compassion traditionally connected with mission today needs to develop in a new direction. People are in the periphery because they are excluded from community. They are excluded from communion with others; excluded from participation, from dignity, from rights. Mission, then, is the effort at inclusion, namely to overcome all forms of exclusion and bring people into communities of equals. Such a mission has to struggle against forces that practice exclusion for various reasons: It could be to maintain purity against pollution; it could be to maintain caste or gender superiority. No one understands exclusion better than poor migrants. They are not included in the community, are set aside, stigmatised and denied human dignity and rights. Today, we need to build up inclusive communities. This is the ultimate guarantee for the practice of human dignity and rights. Creation of inclusive communities applies to both the Church and society.

In our world of globalisation and market, with competition as the driving force, the poor get neglected. Once the poor were treated badly, but their work was wanted by society, by industry, etc. Today, the worst plight of the poor is that they are not wanted. They are viewed as redundant and even a burden. We note in these times of globalisation and advanced capitalism that there is a general diminishing of social consciousness at all levels. The mission of the Church today is to go against the dominant trends and foreground the cause of the poor and the marginalised sections of society. The poor in the understanding of the New Testament are those who are so, because they have been excluded from community. At the root of poverty, then, is the practice of exclusion. How can the mission of the Church become a mission for inclusion of the excluded?

This can be done by creating opportunities for the poor who lack social and cultural capital and by bringing them into new networks of relationships. The new mission should be seen in the struggle against casteism, which is the mother of all exclusions in our country. An inclusive community is one in which the hierarchy of caste does not have a place. But then, we know how much caste hierarchy is there in society and in churches themselves. Purification of the Church from casteism will be an important condition for the effectiveness of the Church's mission in our country.

## Conclusion

Today's world suffers from lack of vision. There is a lot of technology and science, but the absence of a vision for the world, for society and for the well-being of humankind and nature is going to be rather costly. That applies to mission as well. Mission without the vision of the Reign of God could become a religious zealotry that could cause damage to peace and harmony in society and the well-being of one and all. An enlightened approach to mission is what is called for. Such a mission will be one that will be attentive to the context, to the issues and questions affecting society and to the people amidst whom it takes place. It comes to them not as something alien but something that helps and enhances life in its various forms and expressions.

Our reflections have shown the new challenges and frontiers of mission and the need for a renewed praxis. This praxis is both incarnate and prophetic in character. Mission could take place without foregrounding the Christian identity moving beyond the borders of all kinds. It implies learning, overcoming the teaching complex and creating inclusive communities.

The spirit of this kind of mission of the Reign of God is embodied in the praxis of some of the outstanding religious personalities of our times who pursued mission in innovative ways. Martin Luther King, Bishop Desmond Tutu of South Africa, Bishop Belo of East Timor and Mother Theresa of Kolkata were acknowledged through Nobel Prize for Peace—not for teaching the truths of Christianity and its tradition, but for what they did to humankind, to the well-being of society and the world at large. Dalai Lama was acknowledged not for what he did to promote the Buddhist community. He was acknowledged for what he contributed to peace, justice and harmony in the world by drawing on Buddhist tradition and his religious experience of Enlightenment. Christian Mission does not depend on how loud we preach Jesus Christ as the saviour of the world; it happens when we draw from his life and teachings those things that can help the flourishing of life. Ultimately, Christian mission is a discipleship, following the footsteps of Jesus in reaching out and constantly moving towards the Kingdom of God.

*Chapter 2*

# Rethinking the Mission Paradigm in the Light of Emerging Challenges:
## A Critique of the Missional Church

*Kieran Beville*

He who loves his dream of a community more than the Christian community itself becomes a destroyer of the latter, even though his personal intention may be ever so honest and earnest and sacrificial.

– Deitrich Bonhoeffer[1]

There is a movement 'within' the church that is disillusioned with the existing model and methods of traditional church practice. I am not just referring to a restless few who dislike conservative mainstream denominational churches. I am not just referring to people who want to move away from church buildings with pews, elevated pulpits and stained-glass windows. The same attitude is adopted with regard to churches with more modern buildings and more contemporary styles of worship. I am referring to what is known as the missional church.

---

[1] Deitrich Bonhoeffer, *Life Together: A Discussion of Christian Fellowship,* San Francisco, California, Harper One, 1954, p.27.

What is the church? What is its nature and purpose? What is its role in this world? What is its relationship to the wider community? What are its sacred and secular responsibilities? What is a Christian? What is the gospel? What is mission? What is evangelism? In our eagerness to engage with contemporary culture, these questions tend to be neglected. But they come into focus if we try to unite in inter-church collaboration on evangelism. Without broad consensus any such endeavour will be problematic. But we also need a clear understanding of the answers to these questions within our own church community.

Church communities are being drawn into the vortex of unhelpful and unhealthy alliances ostensibly for the sake of evangelism and engagement. These problematic partnerships lead to confusion and compromise. I am concerned that people with evangelistic antennae are picking up this signal on their radar and embarking on a route to nowhere. We need to rethink the mission paradigm in the light of emerging challenges. We need to keep mission central to church life. We need to be in tune with the rhythm of God's heartbeat. But we need biblical perspectives on mission theology as a prerequisite to identifying the way forward. Why? Because there are new directions in mission and it is important to examine these new departures. I want to take the missional church (the most significant new direction in evangelism and engagement) as a case study and offer a critique of this emerging phenomenon by asking whether it is a menace or catalyst.

This article will be more philosophical than methodological and I hope this will not disappoint. I cannot apologise for my approach because I believe good principles provide a foundation for further discussion about the direction we should take and as such is the correct starting place. Perhaps an evangelist or church planter could put flesh on these bones.

The important question to be addressed is whether or not God is at work in this recent phenomenon. Some will say it is the new reality and we better get on board before the ship leaves shore. We cannot simply endorse something just because it is a reality, we must be more discerning and test the spirits. For this we will need some criteria for evaluating a work of the Holy Spirit.

Is the missional church a menace? It is perceived by some as a threat to the welfare of the church. Is it a dangerous development? It seems to me (as a father of three) that new life has a nuisance element to it inasmuch as it disrupts life as it has been heretofore. Certainly, the missional church is a catalyst insofar as it is precipitating change. The question I want to address is: 'Is this change a good thing?' It is a development that has implications not only for missiology but also for Christology and ecclesiology.

The 'attractional' church is understood as a church with a building that is used for regular worship services, prayer meetings, Bible studies, Sunday school, youth group meetings and a host of other programmes and activities. It is argued that in this postmodern culture the 'attractional' church is outmoded. It has been so named because of the idea that the church's missional stance is futile. They see it as ineffective (unsuccessful) because it is based on the hope that people will be attracted to our pews by our preaching and programmes. It might be likened to lighthouses that were once manned and useful but have become irrelevant in a world where seafarers have sophisticated navigation technology based on global positioning systems.

The new movement in evangelism and engagement advocates what it calls 'incarnational' communities. These communities are essentially mission-focused, seeker-centred alternatives to the attractional church model. The locus of mission is re-centred so that instead of expecting un-churched people to come to us we are exhorted to go to them. Clearly, there is much merit in taking such an approach. The exponents of this new way would advocate launching lifeboats rather than building lighthouses as a mission strategy.

So what? At first glance it might sound like nothing more than a different way of fishing for souls. But it is not. This is not a movement that advocates a different way of doing church or merely an attempt to put mission at the centre of church life. If we stay with the nautical analogy for a moment, they would say that doing church differently is like re-arranging the deck chairs on the Titanic. So they see existing attractional church models (our churches) as doomed structures and they are sounding the bell to abandon ship. But are they entering uncharted waters in crafts that will withstand the fury of the raging seas?

There is some concern that some people in this new movement do not have the theological competence to pilot these flimsy vessels. But some of its leaders have advanced theological training and are directors of global networks and are quite organised in their approach to the dissemination of this new thinking through publication, consultation and training. One has to admire the energy of these radical activists. We can be defensive and rigid and reject this new order but that would be as unwise as unquestioningly embracing it. What is needed is an honest, open-minded critique of this movement rather than a gut-feeling response rooted in a predisposed antipathy to anything perceived as novel or trendy.

Has the attractional church passed its 'best before' date? According to the leading exponents of the missional movement, it is time to shut our doors and walk away before the sun sets on the institutionalised church form.

God can and does work in surprising ways and unexpected places as happened in the charismatic movement of the 1960s and 1970s in Ireland and elsewhere. By and large the evangelical community kept its distance because it was problematic and messy. With hindsight we can see that it was a movement where the Holy Spirit was active. It was perceived as a problem but maybe it was an opportunity to provide leadership and discipleship to seekers. I am not saying Christians should have got involved then and I am not sure how we could be involved with some new directions in evangelism and engagement now. But we do need to think about the dynamics of our relationship with the missional church.

According to missional church literature, this movement is seeing people being converted, lives being changed, a searching of the Scriptures and evidence of a new love for God and for one another. Some will say that surely this is to be welcomed and that God does not need our permission to act in unexpected ways. The argument might be offered that, sadly, the Christian establishment is often dragged reluctantly into acknowledging God's work outside its own restricted circles.

## Once upon a time

I once read a story about a lifeboat station on the Eastern Coast of the United States.

> It had begun when some of the locals with sailing experience became concerned about the number of ships that got into trouble in their waters. So they clubbed together and bought a lifeboat. Then they built a boathouse to keep it in. Over the years many lives were saved and there were countless instances of remarkable bravery. Often when the men were out on a rescue, the women would gather at the boathouse, comforting one another as they waited anxiously for news of their husbands. They discovered they worried less if they kept busy, so they put up curtains on the boathouse windows and generally smartened the place up. They persuaded their husbands (when not out on rescues) to put in a little kitchen and some comfortable chairs. Over the years the boathouse became a much more comfortable place to wait. In fact it became so comfortable that the men and their wives used to meet there sometimes when there was no rescuing to be done. Sometimes they brought friends who had never been out in a lifeboat in their lives. Some of the friends moored their yachts nearby. Gradually the character of the lifeboat station changed. One day there was a furious storm and a ship got into trouble just a little way along the coast. The people were all very concerned but no one went out to help. Why? The lifeboat station had become a yacht club.[2]

Many people are now saying that our churches have ceased to be rescue stations for the lost and have become comfortable clubs for the saved.

In fairness to the missional church, which is seeking to create incarnational communities, it must be said that they are well meaning, sincere and hard-working and dedicated to achieving their goals. They rightly understand that there is a problem with regard to reaching the un-churched. They correctly understand that dwindling church attendance and declining numbers of church adherents is a perplexing trend. But because they are evangelists they think that everything in the church should centre round evangelism. I think all believers would want to place huge importance on evangelism but in a balanced way. People with evangelistic antennae have a tendency to develop tunnel vision. The

---

[2] Gary Benfold, 'So that I can rebuild it', *Evangelical Magazine of Wales*, May/June, 2004.

church needs people with these gifts but some blinkered individuals who do not have a panoramic view of the church think that evangelism is all that really matters. I have no doubt that many zealous but theologically naïve individuals are attracted to emerging situations. But I believe the more discerning churches will pick and mix the best and most innovative approaches and this is to be encouraged.

## What is church?

When it comes to understanding the missional church, it is important to examine the biblical basis for Christian community. We all agree that a church is not a building in which Christians meet for worship. Rather the local church consists of a fellowship of believers who gather to worship God. If we do not understand the biblical basis for Christian community, we will be terribly confused about the nature of true fellowship. An obvious concern about the new directions in evangelism and engagement that needs to be addressed is that 'fellowship' with unbelievers is more a kind of camaraderie that does not constitute true unity of the Holy Spirit.

Many church leaders will agree with the missional church's diagnosis concerning the condition of the attractional church in the twenty-first century. But it is their prognosis and prescription that causes some concern. It is important for every generation to find ways of communicating the gospel to its culture but there is a danger that in seeking to be relevant, we cross a line that ought not to be crossed.

## Seeker-centred or seeker-sensitive?

An occupational hazard for evangelists and church planters is that they become seeker-centred (as distinct from seeker-sensitive) and cross the line between contextualisation and syncretism. Contextualisation is about finding ways of explaining and exhibiting the gospel that can be understood within a particular cultural context, without compromising the integrity of the message or the messenger. Syncretism occurs when the desire to be relevant transcends all other motives and both message and messenger become integrated into the prevailing cultural context. Syncretism occurs when Christians adapt, either consciously or unconsciously, to the prevailing worldview. It is the reshaping of Christian beliefs and practices so that they reflect those of the dominant culture. In this process Christianity loses it distinctiveness.[3] Syncretism is frequently birthed from a yearning to make the gospel appear relevant. The church attempts to make its message attractive to outsiders and as these adaptations become regularly assimilated they become an integral part of the church's life. When significant changes in worldview take place, the Christian community, swept along by the ebb and flow of cultural currents, begins to lose her moorings.[4]

There has been a significant paradigm shift best summarised by the word *postmodernism*. Some church people are wondering if it will come into the church. The reality is that it is well embedded in the church. Many churches have gone beyond the process of contextualising the gospel in Western culture and have married themselves to these core values of society. One writer cautions: "While Christian witness must be savvy concerning the realities of the postmodern condition in order to make the historic Christian message understandable and pertinent to denizens of the contemporary world, this does not mean that we should become postmodernists in the process."[5]

## Radical developments

There are many radical developments in how church is practiced today. We are going to see much more of this kind of thoroughgoing recalibration in the next decade. The orientation towards missional and incarnational communities is not merely a rediscovery of the values and vision of the ancient faith communities found in the book of Acts. We must be careful not to disregard centuries of subsequent church history (including the Reformation) as if they are entirely irrelevant. That would be like

---

[3] Gailyn Van Rheenen, "Modern and Postmodern Syncretism in Theology and Missions" in C. Douglas McConnell (ed.), *The Holy Spirit and Mission Dynamics*, Pasadena: Wm. Carey, 1997, p.173.

[4] *Ibid.*, p.173.

[5] Douglas Groothuis, "Facing the Challenge of Postmodernism" in Francis Beckwith, William Lane Craig and J. P. Moreland (eds.), *To Everyone an Answer: A Case for the Christian Worldview*, Downers Grove, Illinois: IVP, 2004, p.253.

throwing the baby out with the bathwater and that is a calamitous thing to do. Has our failure to address mission in a holistic way partly contributed to new departures in evangelism and engagement?[6]

The missional church is not a counter-cultural movement; it is in fact the opposite. Certainly, they react to the consumerist, materialistic and therapeutic values of modernist churches that have developed too cosy a relationship with the prevailing cultural norms. There is a real danger that they will lose their distinct identity as Christians.

The missional church contends that traditional Christian identity is perceived as unattractive to seekers. It charges the church with creating self-serving institutions that are not connecting with community. It would say that the attractional church has merely created holy huddles that are no-go zones for unbelievers who do not feel they belong to these 'clubs.' They say that we have retrenched into our private enclaves. The accusation that we live a kind of neo-monastic existence is nonsense, and this myth needs to be dispelled. Most of our people are connected to the real world in one way or another.

Missional church people integrate themselves into various communities and sub-cultures and intentionally conceal their spiritual identities until they have built what they call, 'meaningful relationships.' I feel there is something inappropriate and dishonest in this kind of subterfuge. I think Christians are called to be conspicuous in this world, not chameleons who adapt to the surrounding environment. We should not be disingenuous about our intentions. Christians are to be *in* the world but not *of* the world. D. L. Moody said, "The ship is meant to be in the water but God help her when the water gets into the ship." It is an obvious truth that states an important principle of Christian living.

The missional church claims to be involved in creating places of inclusive belonging where God's kingdom can be experienced. This sounds good until what that actually means is spelled out. Certainly,

---

[6] I have witnessed holistic models of mission working well in India and Eastern Europe but I acknowledge the dangers inherent in this model whereby the gospel message of salvation can become subordinate to material concerns.

Christians should be creating places of welcome but we should not adopt an 'end-justifies-the-means' approach to winning souls. The church is the bride of Christ and should remain pure and uncompromised.

Some new directions in evangelism and engagement are manifestations of a myopic movement that appeals to the disaffected and trend-orientated. Any critique of their motives and methods is viewed with suspicion and deemed to be judgemental. They dismiss people who present a different theological perspective as those who, 'know too much, talk too much and judge too much.'[7] This is both unfair and unhelpful.

The missional church criticism of the attractional church is rooted in the observation that there are so few conversions. They say churches are, 'musty, fussy, clubby, judgmental, mean, punishing, ungenerous...'[8] It is an unfair generalisation to have the faithful and fervent work of so many pastors, elders, deacons and church members denigrated in this way. Yet we must examine ourselves to see if there is an element of truth in this.

However, I think the missional church tends to see 'growth' in narrow terms, as an increase in numbers. But growth in a church context is not just about people coming to faith but also about people growing to maturity as individuals and growing together in unity and love as a community and numerical growth may be a part of this process.

## Schismatic squabble

Differences about how evangelism and engagement are to be conducted have the potential to give rise to schismatic squabbles. I do not want to contribute to polemical 'debate' but new directions have potentially dangerous undercurrents and I think it would be negligent not to flag this. Our desire to engage with contemporary culture must have safeguards against being ensnared by it. Otherwise many who start out meaning well might end up watching Oprah, Larry King or Dr. Phil for spiritual guidance.

---

[7] Hugh Halter and Matt Smay, *The Tangible Kingdom*, p.xxii.
[8] *Ibid.*, p.11.

What are we to make of pastors leaving churches to become baristas and barmen in the belief that in so doing they will be more effective witnesses for Christ? I suggest that people who do this were never ideally suited to pastoral ministry. Rather, they were church planters and evangelists. I wish them well but hope their new mission outpost situations will stay connected to local church communities.

For the missional church connecting with sojourners is paramount. They establish communities that permit anybody, irrespective of belief or behaviour, to belong. It appears to have a disregard for doctrine and tradition and argues that we should set aside our apologetics and theology and include those outside the kingdom. Church communities must be places of benevolence and blessing. We must extend a warm and genuine welcome to all. However, the theological and biblical reality is that one does not belong to Christ until and unless one has repented of one's sin and confessed Christ as Saviour. We should not pretend that people belong when in fact they do not. That would be deceptive and unwise. It is like allowing people to come to our homes and dine with us. We can have a great deal of interaction but they are not members of our family.

Some new directions in mission tend to have an end-justifies-the-means approach to involving non-believers in church ministries. This has resulted in incidents such as stoned and drunk musicians playing at their gatherings and the unconverted teaching Bible stories to children. Boundaries are blurred and nobody in their communities is bothered by this.

Because society has lost interest in 'organised Christendom' there is a desire to offer it a radical alternative. An important question, therefore, is whether or not this 'alternative' is authentic to the ideals of Scripture.

The missional church seems to have lost confidence in the efficacy of preaching to accomplish God's purposes. Maybe they have been exposed to poor models of preaching, and sadly there is much of that about. I believe that preaching Christ in a postmodern culture is not only feasible but imperative.[9] The missional church argues that people

---

[9] This needs to be glossed and interacted upon with keen sense of missional commitment.

will not change by listening to preaching. I wonder why Jesus preached. Jesus was first and foremost a preacher. The Nazareth Manifesto identifies preaching as central to his ministry. If we want to model him, we cannot dismiss preaching. Even by their own admission the missional church says that 'Christology determines missiology, and missiology determines ecclesiology.'[10] The whole notion of church is being systematically deconstructed and radically redefined.

## To boldly go where no man has gone before

The missional desire to spend time with the un-churched is admirable. They see themselves as pioneers who are taking risks in going, 'where no man has gone before.' For them the fulfilment of the Great Commission to 'go' is not merely about outreach evangelism programmes, rather it is about living among and belonging. But we must love the found as well as the lost. To what extent, if any, have we contributed to the sense of disaffection that is giving rise to this movement by inserting extra-biblical proscriptions, written and unwritten (about issues like alcohol, smoking, styles of dress, etc.), as conditions of membership in constitutions and codes of conduct?

It is difficult to get the balance right between being a community that confronts the godless values of the cultural norms and being an inclusive community. The missional church is calling for a revolution in inclusive community in which the masses will want to participate. The distaste for present forms of church is evident in the words of Hugh Halter: "The typical message has been to be good, stop sinning, go to church, and wait for God to come back. Yuck. It's too simple."[11] Surely, it is right to stop sinning. Sin is grievously offensive to God, and to cease sinning is an indication that the person has newness of life. This is what God wants and expects of converts. Is it not right to go to a place where like-minded people assemble to worship God as a community of believers? Did not the early church have an eschatological hope that radically altered how it lived?

---

[10] Michael Frost and Alan Hirsch, *The Shaping of Things to Come*, p.16.

[11] Hugh Halter and Matt Smay, *The Tangible Kingdom*, p.74.

The missional church believes that through benevolent action in the community spiritual dialogue will ensue and so they openly admit that they would prefer do something useful (like sweeping up leaves in the community) on Sunday morning instead of going to church. They will randomly cancel their gatherings so that they can do something alternative to 'worship.' But the kingdom of God is not about winning the 'Tidy Towns' competition! Some churches have involved their youth in making a positive contribution to the community by clearing up litter. This kind of activity can be very positive and can open doors of opportunity to conversations about how our faith motivates us to do good deeds. The problem is in conducting such benevolent acts as *alternatives* to church worship services. The missional church does not seem to care much if people attend their Sabbath gatherings. They encourage people to spend their Sunday mornings being with sojourners. Perhaps the missional church is attractive because one does not have to forsake much or believe much in order to belong to it.

The missional church talks about *apprenticing* disciples as more authentic than *cognitive* discipleship. But Jesus taught his disciples for three years and the Great Commission instructs us to "teach" all that Christ has taught. This is clearly part of the discipleship process. Maybe the discipleship process is best done through supervised hands-on experience supplemented with teaching.

In his trenchant analysis of the cultural corruption weakening the church's thought and witness, David Wells argues that evangelicals have blurred the distinctions between Christ and culture and have largely abandoned their traditional emphasis on divine transcendence in favour of an emphasis on divine immanence. In doing so, they have produced a faith in God that is of little consequence to those who believe. He says that 'there is a profound sense in which the church has to be "otherworldly."'[12]

---

[12] David F. Wells, *God in the Wasteland: The Reality of Truth in a World of Fading Dreams*, Wm. B. Eerdmans, Grand Rapids: Michigan, and Inter-Varsity Press, Leicester, England, 1994, p.41.

Nobody is saying that everything in existing structures and the prevailing *modus operandi* is sacrosanct. We must be open to the idea of reviewing our structures to see if they hinder or help our goals. But all of this must be done in the light of Scripture. In this new movement, church becomes a discovery zone for participating sojourners where the desire to be relevant leads to convictions being diluted. We must be careful about how we proceed so that what is harmful can be rejected and what is helpful can be retained as we seek to advance in evangelism and engagement.

## Evaluating criteria

Are there any criteria that can be used to evaluate contemporary approaches to mission? What is a genuine work of the Holy Spirit? One would certainly hesitate to make unfair accusations or derive inappropriate conclusions about any activity that might be authentic. John MacArthur has presented material condensed, adapted and excerpted from Jonathan Edwards', "The Distinguishing Marks of a Work of the Spirit of God."[13] This MacArthur/Edwards article identifies five distinguishing characteristics of the Holy Spirit's work based on an analysis of 1 John 4:1-8. These are helpful in determining whether or not emerging trends are a true work of God. MacArthur says that a genuine work of the Holy Spirit exalts the true Christ, opposes Satan's interests, points people to the Scriptures, elevates truth and results in love for God and others. Let us examine the new phenomenon in the light of this standard.

First, we must ask if the missional church upholds a Scriptural view of Christ. Clearly, the doctrine of the incarnation must be affirmed. The missional church subscribes to this truth in asserting that Jesus is the Son of God.[14] This community of believers (and I think that is, generally, what they are) genuinely desire to lead people to Christ. Christ is revered (perhaps sentimentally) in this new movement.

---

[13] 'A True Work of the Spirit', © John MacArthur, Jr, 'Grace to You'. See also: http://www.biblebb.com/files/edwards/je-marksofhs.htm

[14] As far as I am aware they believe in the sinless life, substitutionary death/atonement, resurrection, ascension, intercessory role, divinity, trinity and second coming of Christ.

Nevertheless, there is something imaginary about the Christ they extol. I have already asserted that Jesus was a preacher. The missional church makes a distinction between 'Galilean' Christians and 'Jerusalem' Christians. The Galilean Christians are those who interpret the Bible through the life of Jesus. The Jerusalem Christians are more doctrinal. This bias towards the Galilean way is quite subjective. They see Jerusalem people as idolaters of the Bible who have overly intellectualised spirituality. They have reduced the Bible to the gospels and argue that if we only had the gospels, Christianity would look very different today. But we have the entire canon of Scripture because God wanted to reveal more than what is disclosed in the gospels. Their tendency to ignore, reject or devalue any Scripture that is not directly spoken by Jesus is potentially heretical.

Second, a distinguishing mark of a work of the Spirit of God is that it will oppose Satan's interests. Satan desires that people remain in a sinful condition and succumb to the lusts of the flesh. The missional church is not entirely indifferent to sinfulness but its attitude to sin is lax. I am not saying they are dens of iniquity. They claim to create an environment in which the conscience can become sensitive to the truth in relation to sin. But in the absence of preaching about the dreadfulness of sin, they have created an environment that is casual about sin.

The third mark that distinguishes a work of the Spirit of God is that it points people to the Scriptures. The missional church does not induce a high a regard for the whole counsel of God. As already mentioned, they tend to be red-letter people rather than biblical people. In other words, they put a higher value on the words of Christ than on the words of other authors of Scripture. This distorts revelation.

The fourth feature of a work of the Spirit of God is that it elevates truth. Certainly, the missional church makes people more aware of the central gospel truths. They may be effective in leading people to faith but fall short of leading them to maturity in Christ.

The fifth and final mark that distinguishes a work of the Spirit of God is that it results in love for God and others. The missional church loves the lost and it is to be highly commended for this. They profess to love God and I do not doubt their sincerity in this regard. Nevertheless, the God they profess to love is eviscerated of much of the divine nature as a sin-loathing God.

The missional church is not heretical but it is a movement that has potentially harmful effects. Nevertheless, in spite of reservations about and objections to its 'unorthodox' irregularities and potential hazards, it cannot be dismissed as a work of Satan. Must it, therefore, be embraced as a work of the Holy Spirit? From past experience (consider the history of revival movements) it is clear that the Spirit of God can work even in the midst of much that might be deemed 'problematic.'

We should be very reluctant, therefore, to condemn a work in which the Holy Spirit might be involved and we should have a similar sense of hesitancy about contributing to the polarisation of differing Christian communities. But we must test the spirits and where we find deficiencies and dangers, we must be diligent in alerting others to the potential pitfalls.

**The way forward**

One's ideas about mission are shaped by one's theology. Much has been written in recent years about mission, which focuses on methodological approaches to engaging contemporary culture. Many of these works boldly propose new ways of engaging with contemporary culture. We must be concerned about keeping mission central to church life and identifying a way forward in the labyrinthine complexity of postmodern society.

The trendy literature suggests that the 'attractional' model of the church of Christendom is outmoded. It is an influential body of work that contends that what is needed now is a 'missional' and 'incarnational' Christian church. But these works tend to be primarily focused on how to engage in mission rather than putting in place a theological foundation that would underpin the missionary enterprise. What is needed is a biblical perspective on mission theology that informs and shapes our understanding, approaches and methodologies in facing the unfinished task of 'making disciples of all nations.' This will not only safeguard and strengthen mission but also provide a means of evaluating trends that seek to influence future directions in mission activity.

Postmodernism presents a new frontier situation. We must have a missionary impulse to bear witness to the gospel. Certainly, we must adapt to the new environment but without compromising. We live with the tension of seeking ways of contextualising the gospel without capitulating to culture. As the current cultural context is emerging we are in uncharted waters and navigating our way will require experienced and savvy people at the helm.

## Paradigm shift

It is generally acknowledged now that a paradigm shift has taken place. This 'cultural sea change' has contributed to significantly widening the gulf between the church and culture.[15] This is not necessarily a bad thing because the Western church has had too cosy a relationship with the prevailing culture. We now have to talk not about 'culture' but 'cultures' because we live in what might be called a 'pluriverse' rather than a 'universe.' In this kaleidoscopic cultural context, we are all influenced by a variety of cultures in diet, dress, art, architecture, music and the media. Secularisation, cultural and religious pluralism, globalisation, advances in technology have all impacted on the church's role in society. It is not just city centre churches that have this *mélange* of cultures but rural churches as well. It is in response to such challenges that new directions and departures in evangelism and engagement have emerged.

Navigating this emerging missiological landscape will involve experimenting with approaches to ministry that will challenge present understandings of what it means to be the church today. These challenges are new opportunities to engage in innovative forms of communication and dialogue. Should we consider this taking place in unconventional spaces, often referred to as 'the third place'? This would mean inhabiting places outside church buildings that are also inhabited by people of other faiths. The missional church thinks in terms of shared space rather than sacred space. They see our commitment to buildings as an absurd loyalty akin to the captain going down with the sinking ship. Evangelists and

---

[15] Graham Ward, "Introduction: 'Where We Stand'", in Graham Ward (ed.), *The Blackwell Companion to Postmodern Theology*, Oxford and Malden, Mass.; Blackwell Publishers, 2001, p.xv.

theologians must work together like architects and engineers in constructing a new order that is both attractive and safe.

## Being church today

So, what does it mean to be the church today? It is about participating in a way of life. It means an understanding that we are the gathered community of God's people. We gather around Christ and a body of divinity, indwelt by the Holy Spirit, united as blood-brothers. We can create all sorts of artificial communities but the church is an organism, not an organisation. It is a living, dynamic and organic entity of the redeemed.

The missional church challenges believers to leave their private enclaves and comfort zones and infiltrate unorthodox and even profane places. But discernment is needed. Some will reject the call out of hand as an invitation to compromise, which can only result in Christians being contaminated. Others will rush in 'where angels fear to tread.'

When visiting a city, it is helpful to find the map that says 'you are here' accompanied by a big arrow pointing to the spot. We can navigate from there. With regard to evangelism and engagement, there is a sense in which the landscape does not change and the map does not change but we need to know where we are and re-orientate the map so that we can head in the right direction.

Evangelism is not an elective element of the spiritual life. These new approaches to evangelism and engagement have far-reaching implications because they are not proposing prioritising mission within existing church structures. It is not about churches giving more time to mission or conducting outreach more often. It is not about preaching more about mission or having more missionaries come and speak in the local church. It is not about more time being given to prayer for mission. It is, rather, a 'complete reorientation of the church, a reshaping of its life, a rediscovery of mission as the activity around which everything else is coordinated.'[16]

---

[16] Michael Frost, *Encounter with God*: Scripture Union Bible Reading Notes, July-Sept., 2010, p.45.

## Emerging phenomenon

In the West, we are now living in what may be called the post-Christendom era. Many people are no longer interested in what the church has to offer. Paradoxically, in postmodern culture, there is a new openness to spirituality. In this situation, where the church in its present institutionalised form is perceived as irrelevant, growing numbers of Christians are engaging in more innovative missionary activity. But the stories gathered from these emergent church projects give rise to some concern about the future direction of mission. These spirited experiments are primarily motivated by a desire, within the church, to be more relevant to society in the twenty-first-century. This relatively new movement is not comprised merely of armchair theorists. Rather, this is a radicalised and organised cohort of activists who are effectively disseminating their message, recruiting adherents and replicating missional communities in Western society.

The missional church is an expression of the emerging church phenomenon. It de-emphasises what it perceives as 'divisive' doctrine by emphasising the primacy of relationship. This is characteristically postmodern. They also elevate God's (almost indiscriminate) love for mankind over his essential holiness. By raising unity above truth, the missional church creates an atmosphere where peace is the *summum bonum*, that is, the supreme good from which all others are derived.

The missional church is essentially rooted in contemporary culture and this fact may be the cause of its own demise. Philosophies that are driven by culture are inexorably destined to disappear in time. As Os Guinness warned, "He who marries the spirit of the age soon becomes a widower."[17]

The greatest threats to the health of the church are liberalism, on the one hand, and legalism, on the other. The *avant-garde* are the adventurers and innovators who pioneer new approaches and departures. They are more likely to gravitate to liberalism than legalism. The missional

---

[17] Os Guinness, *Dining with the Devil*, Grand Rapids: Baker, 1993. I have been informed that Google References attributes this remark to W. R. Inge, the famed Dean of St Paul's Cathedral.

church mentality is compatible with this instinct. The rearguard, however, is comprised of those whose instinct is conservative and whose desire is to protect and preserve the status quo and as such they are more likely to gravitate to legalism. I think we all have a default mode in this regard.

Faith should not be inert and unchanging rather it should be dynamic and vibrant. Our experiences of life must inspire reflection and our interaction with others who hold different views ought to stimulate honest appraisal and reappraisal of our own opinions and positions. Daniel Migliore says:

> ...theology must be critical reflection on the community's faith and practice...not simply a reiteration of what has been or is currently believed and practiced by a community of faith. It is a quest for truth, and that presupposes that the proclamation and practice of the community of faith are always in need of examination and reform...When this responsibility is neglected....the faith of the community is invariably threatened by shallowness, arrogance and ossification[18]

Those with a risk-taking disposition want to face the white-water rapids in a canoe. Those with a conservative bias would prefer to take a trip in a barge on the canal. It is unlikely that those with a risk-taking disposition and those with a conservative bias will enjoy a journey together. The disposition of the reformers at the time of the Reformation was not conservative. This may be a surprise to those who revere the reformers as establishment heroes. We must cherish a past that is not only connected to the present but also connected to the future.

At the outset, I asked if the missional church was a menace or a catalyst. I believe it is both. The words of Mr. Spock might be applied to the missional church: "It's life, Jim, but not as we know it."

Our theoretical presuppositions about mission and our theological rationale for mission should be determined by the Word of God. We must allow Scripture to speak for itself as the missionary manual rather than impose our views upon it. Eric Wright says:

---

[18] Daniel L. Migliore, *Faith Seeking Understanding: An Introduction to Christian Theology*, Grand Rapids, Michigan: Eerdmans, 1996, p. xxi.

Nothing can be more important than to ensure that our missionary presuppositions reflect the principles of Scripture. This will not be true if theology is ignored, because theology brings us face to face with the principles, parameters and priorities that God has revealed.[19]

Mission must be a Christ-centred intentional process of communicating the gospel in word and deed. An informed biblical missional view goes beyond the frequently quoted commissioning passages to a more comprehensive perspective from Genesis to Revelation. Nevertheless, the missionary mandate is about living out the Great Commission with the passion of the Great Commandment (to make disciples and love God and neighbour). Christ's followers are to take the gospel to all peoples (nations and ethnic groups) irrespective of class, culture or creed. This demands conviction, commitment and courage in the face of the objections of pluralism and the hostility of anti-Christian fundamentalisms. Christians must avoid the pitfall of theological liberalism, which perceives evangelism as proselytising. Christians must also avoid the snare of religious legalism, which is nurtured in separatist enclaves.

Our God is a missionary God. The Bible is a missionary book. The church is a missionary institution. Christ's mandate is a missionary mandate. The Great Commandment (to love) is to be the regulating principle of all mission activity. Contemporary culture presents many opportunities for the entrance of the gospel. So each church must find ways of having meaningful interaction with those outside the church. But this must be done without capitulating to the prevailing culture.

The missional church may be over zealous in its approach and naïve in much of its activity but it has led to some innovative ways of engaging with culture. However, its central problem is its overemphasis on pragmatism. A. W. Tozer identified this issue as far back as 1955 when he said, "Religious pragmatism is running wild among the orthodox. Truth is whatever works. If it gets results, it is good."[20]

---

[19] Eric E. Wright, *A Practical Theology of Missions: Dispelling the Mystery; Recovering the Passion*, DayOne, UK, 2010, p.10.

[20] A. W. Tozer, *The Root of the Righteous*, Harrisburgh, PA: Christian Publications, 1955, p.8.

Eric Wright suggests that "the most pragmatic thing we can do in the long run is to teach what God has revealed, trust his revealed methods and try to apply them in dependence on the Holy Spirit."[21]

Our involvement in the world comes about in a variety of natural and intentional ways. One of the most obvious is in the workplace (though, for pastors, this might be a problem because our world is inhabited by Christians). There are other areas where the Christian may come in contact with the world, such as sports, cultural pursuits, social activities, volunteering, educational programmes and local or national politics.

Scripture refers to anyone involved in any form of government as 'God's servant' (Rom. 13:4). God has ordained the powers that be (Rom. 13:10). Clearly, the Christian individual may, in good conscience, be involved in politics. The Old Testament character Daniel walked with God and occupied a senior position in the Babylonian/Persian civil service. Another Old Testament character, Joseph, was directly involved in the government of Egypt. Clearly, therefore, God's people are not forbidden to be involved in society. Some Christians have spearheaded important social reform, such as William Wilberforce, with the abolition of slavery.

There are many practical and positive ways in which we can let our light shine. Our good deeds give credibility to the gospel message we proclaim. The Christian is to be concerned for good works as well as good words. If we are to model the master, we must realise that he was compassionate and went about doing good (Acts 10:38).

But there is a difference between humanitarianism and Christian mission. Therefore, we need to ensure that we engage in more than philanthropy. The essential difference is the gospel message of salvation. Christian mission ministers to the soul of humanity and its greatest need: that of a Saviour. We must distinguish between the calling of the Christian citizen to engage in social and political action and the mandate of the church. Nevertheless, in certain contexts, the gospel has unavoidable political implications.

---

[21] Eric E. Wright, *Op. cit.* p.10.

Jesus could have gained enormous popularity if he had been willing to respond to the people's political agenda but he resisted. We must do likewise by resisting such temptations and being alert to the danger of being used to further the world's agenda, even when aspects of that agenda are good causes. History abounds with sad examples of the church being hijacked in this way. Para-church organisations, which started out with an overtly Christian mission, have drifted from their formative ideals and have become virtually secularised; for example, the Salvation Army and the Y.M.C.A.

One of the major dangers facing the Christian church in contemporary culture is religious pluralism. The missionary frontier is the line that separates belief from unbelief. That means that it is also the line between false and true religion where cherished beliefs are challenged, contradicted or even, when necessary, condemned. With regard to the latter, the practice of *sati* in the Indian context was identified by William Carey as morally wrong.

It is important that the Bible should be respected in any shaping of things to come, because it is the authoritative source of our understanding of evangelism and engagement. The church's mission is about presenting the unique and universal claims of Jesus and that runs counter to the pluralist agenda. The church's mission is about calling people to repentance, faith and community relationship. We are partners in this great work in progress. Consider the challenging words of the well-known hymn:

### Facing a Task Unfinished [22]

*Facing a task unfinished*
*That drives us to our knees*
*A need that, undiminished*
*Rebukes our slothful ease*

---

[22] Frank Houghton (1894-1972), in Paul E. G. Cook and Graham Harrison (eds.), *Christian Hymns*, Evangelical Movement of Wales, 1977.

We, who rejoice to know Thee
Renew before Thy throne
The solemn pledge we owe Thee
To go and make Thee known

Where other lords beside Thee
Hold their unhindered sway
Where forces that defied Thee
Defy Thee still today
With none to heed their crying
For life, and love, and light
Unnumbered souls are dying
And pass into the night

We bear the torch that flaming
Fell from the hands of those
Who gave their lives proclaiming
That Jesus died and rose
Ours is the same commission
The same glad message ours
Fired by the same ambition
To Thee we yield our powers

O Father who sustained them
O Spirit who inspired
Saviour, whose love constrained them
To toil with zeal untired
From cowardice defend us
From lethargy awake!
Forth on Thine errands send us
To labour for Thy sake.

Chapter 3

# Rhythm of God's Heartbeat
## Biblical Perspectives on Mission Theology
### Kieran Beville

Our theoretical presuppositions about mission and our theological rationale for mission should be determined by the Word of God. We must allow Scripture to speak for itself as the missionary manual rather than impose our views upon it. Understanding the rhythm of God's heartbeat is about being in tune with his heart and being in touch with what he is doing in contemporary culture. Being missional minded is about seeing as God sees, feeling as God feels and acting as God acts. The heart of God demonstrates that he is a missionary God, seeking to reach a world separated from him.

The apostle John said, "For God so loved the world, that he gave his only Son, that whoever believes in him should not perish but have eternal life" (John 3:16). This tells us much about the heart of God and the quality of that perfect, sacrificial love.

If the world is to be reached for Christ, we need to share God's heart desire. God is the first and greatest missionary and all of Scripture bears testimony to that. The Bible is the revelation of his unfolding endeavours to reach and redeem the lost. We must begin to realise that mission is not just based on a few proof texts of Scripture rather it is rooted in the compassionate heart of God and evident in all his activity with humanity. Robert Speer comments on the great commission:

> The last command of Christ is not the deep and final ground of the church's missionary duty. That duty is authoritatively stated in the words of the great commission, and it is of infinite consequence to have had it so stated by our Lord Himself. But if these particular words had never been spoken by Him, or if, having been spoken, they had not been preserved, the missionary duty of the church would not be in the least affected. The supreme arguments for missions are not found in any specific words. It is in the very being and character of God that the deepest ground of the missionary enterprise is to be found.[1]

It is good to read books about mission; to have an interest in mission; to be excited about mission; to be stimulated by mission stories; but we need to be aroused from our inertia and motivated to engage in mission.

Christians are to be *in* the world but not *of* the world. Jesus said:

> I have given them your word, and the world has hated them because they are not of the world, just as I am not of the world. I do not ask that you take them out of the world, but that you keep them from the evil one. They are not of the world, just as I am not of the world (John 17:14-16)

In speaking of 'the world', Jesus is speaking of people who are not in right relationship with God. We do and must have contact with the world. The Christian cannot and should not be cloistered away from outsiders. But we tend to get into holy huddles where we become comfortable with our lives of seclusion. These spiritual enclaves are a kind of neo-monastic existence. But we must not withdraw from the world for fear of contamination.

We regularly interact with the world in the workplace where we have opportunity to bear testimony to the grace of God in word and deed. We can bring a Christian perspective to bear in conversations about social and spiritual issues as opportunity allows.

---

[1] Cited in George W. Peters, *A Biblical Theology of Missions*, Chicago: Moody, 1972, p.55.

When Paul told the Corinthian church not to associate with sexually immoral people, he was not referring to people of the world. If that was the case, we would all have to leave the world. He was forbidding the Christian to fellowship with professing Christians who were slipping into immorality, drunkenness or idolatry.

Our example in all things is Christ. He ate with tax collectors and sinners (Matt. 9:11), and the religious leaders of the day grumbled about that (Luke 19:7). But the writer to the Hebrews informs us that Christ was, "holy, innocent, unstained, separated from sinners" (Heb. 7:26). In the same way, as Jesus was not of the world his disciples are not of the world. So the permission and privilege of involvement in the world must be balanced with the obligation to be a distinctive community. We should not live according to the values of the world. Our priorities are to be fundamentally different and distinctive. This may bring criticism because people of other faiths will resent it when Christians do not join in sinful activity. Thus, we may expect a backlash. Peter commented on this:

> For the time that is past suffices for doing what the Gentiles want to do, living in sensuality, passions, drunkenness, orgies, drinking parties, and lawless idolatry. With respect to this they are surprised when you do not join them in the same flood of debauchery, and they malign you (1 Pet. 4:3-4).

I wonder how many believers today are maligned for not participating in dubious social practices. We are not to be materialistic by indulging in the carnival of consumerism. We are not to be hedonistic in a heathen world.

But there is a difference between the work of secular development agencies and Christian mission. It is not merely that the Christian is motivated by faith. There are Christian charities and mission societies that have a distinctively Christian ethos. The Christian does not have a monopoly on love, compassion, morality and charity. Many non-Christian organisations (either secular or religious) engage in tremendous work for the poor and the marginalised of this world. But there is a difference between humanitarianism and Christian mission. We need to ensure that we engage in more than philanthropy. The essential difference is the gospel message of salvation. Christian mission ministers to the soul of humanity and its greatest need: that of a Saviour.

The Gospel of John relates how Jesus on one occasion, moved with compassion, healed the sick and fed five thousand people. The crowds wished to make him king, undoubtedly supposing he would redress the injustices of the Roman occupation. But Jesus withdrew from them and later told them to seek food that endures to eternal life (John 6:14-15, 25-27). Certain sections of evangelicalism identify this as a text that teaches that the church's mission is *essentially* spiritual and *incidentally* material. In other words the Church's duty is to communicate the gospel message of salvation and lead people to faith in Christ and anything else is *relatively* unimportant. According to this view, social action is not essential to the church's role and is, therefore supplementary. These people will argue that Christ's priority was spiritual, not physical.

Though Christian mission may have (indeed should have) a humanitarian dimension, it is not humanitarianism. Mission is not essentially about development in the sense that it is not about bringing the benefits of the developed world to the underdeveloped or developing world; though that may be a consequence or outcome of mission activity, it is not the motivating factor. Neither is it the benchmark for determining the success of missionary endeavour. Mission is not a process of civilising or westernising other cultures. It is not a means of socialisation. Christ's followers are to continue his work of taking the gospel to all peoples (nations and ethnic groups) irrespective of class, culture or creed. There is a danger that mission may be perceived as the spiritual colonisation of non-Christian cultures. This politicises and polarises communities and gives impetus to polemical rhetoric and nationalistic resistance.

Sometimes those who cross geographical and cultural boundaries to preach the gospel where Christ is not known (or where little is known of Christ) are insensitive or indifferent to the new environment. Often it is not the message of the gospel that offends but the method of disseminating it.

The truth is that most Christians are not living for Christ but for themselves. Paul challenges the Corinthian believers with these words, "and he died for all, that those who live might no longer live for themselves but for him who for their sake died and was raised" (2 Cor. 5:15). Just as Christ was completely obedient to his Father's will and just as Paul lived solely for God's purposes and glory so we too must live for God. Is this too high a calling? Is this fanaticism? Is this just for Jesus and Paul and an elite group of devotees? Or is this the attitude that God wants from all of us? I think we know the answer to these questions. We need to forsake self-centred living for the sake of the kingdom of God.

Christ's mandate to us is a missionary mandate: "As the Father has sent me, even so I am sending you" (John 20:21). If we are to keep mission central to church life, we must keep it central to our preaching and programmes. We must not allow mission to be perceived as something peripheral. We must dispel the notion that mission is an optional extra for Christians. It is not an elective element of the spiritual life rather it is (or ought to be) the core constituent of faithful living.

Mission did not begin with the incarnation. Christ's first coming was not plan 'B' to redress the fall of man. The missionary heart of God and his missionary purpose are revealed from Genesis, right throughout the Old and New Testaments up to the book of Revelation.

To some, the Great Commission is the only known reference to the subject of mission in Scripture. Certainly, it marks a turning point in redemptive history where the Messiah's kingdom had dawned in new power. But it is not the beginning of mission. There is an interesting connection between the opening and closing of Matthew's gospel. Matthew opens his gospel account with the genealogy of Christ in the line of Abraham and David: "The book of the genealogy of Jesus Christ, the son of David, the son of Abraham" (Matt. 1:1-2). This reference to Abraham at the beginning of Mathew's gospel reminds us of the promise that through Abraham's offspring, "all the nations of the earth shall be blessed" (Gen. 26:4). When we look at this promise, it is clear that God was or is interested in the rest of the world as well. In the closing words of Matthew's gospel, we find Jesus sending his disciples to all nations: "All authority in heaven and on earth has been given to me. Go therefore and make disciples of all nations, baptizing them in the name of the Father and of the Son and of the Holy Spirit, teaching them to observe all that I have commanded you. And behold, I am with you always, to the end of the age" (Matt. 28:18-20).

In order to trace mission in the Old Testament, it might be helpful to think of a piece of orchestral music. Often the composer will weave a motif through the whole work, which is recognisable from time to time. This is the essence of the piece. It might be introduced by the violins, picked up later by the oboes and again included in the brass section. Each time we hear it we say, "There it is again!" In a similar way, the mission motif is woven into Scripture. Abraham was the father of the Jews, God's chosen people. They were chosen to be a light to all nations. Initially, God chose a man and extended the blessing to his family, his clan, his tribe, all twelve tribes and now, through Christ, to Abraham's offspring, the blessing is extended to all nations. The blessings of salvation were never intended only for the Jews. God's ultimate plan includes all nations, every tribe and tongue.

So right from the first book of the Bible the desire of God's heart (that all nations of the earth will be blessed with the message of salvation) is clearly expressed. Here we see the first note in that motif being struck. This is the keynote. This motif was to be heard again and again at the most critical times in redemptive history. The blessing promised not only *to* but *through* Abraham was for all nations. This blessing was to be received through Christ. It is received through faith:

> Just as Abraham 'believed God, and it was counted to him as righteousness.' Know then that it is those of faith who are the sons of Abraham. And the Scripture, foreseeing that God would justify the Gentiles by faith, preached the gospel beforehand to Abraham, saying, 'In you shall all the nations be blessed.' So then, those who are of faith are blessed along with Abraham, the man of faith (Gal. 3:6-9).

Look at how Solomon prays for non-Jews who visit the temple:

> Likewise, when a foreigner, who is not of your people Israel, comes from a far country for your name's sake (for they shall hear of your great name and your mighty hand, and of your outstretched arm), when he comes and prays toward this house, hear in heaven your dwelling place and do according to all for which the foreigner calls to you, in order that all the peoples of the earth may know your name and fear you, as do your people

Israel, and that they may know that this house that I have built is called by your name. (1 Kings 8:41-43).

See how this is similar to a declaration in Isaiah

> And the foreigners who join themselves to the Lord, to minister to him, to love the name of the Lord, and to be his servants, everyone who keeps the Sabbath and does not profane it, and holds fast my covenant—these I will bring to my holy mountain, and make them joyful in my house of prayer; their burnt offerings and their sacrifices will be accepted on my altar; for my house shall be called a house of prayer for all peoples (Isa. 56:6-7).

Mission is what the Bible is all about. Mission is the church in motion to the rhythm of God's heartbeat. God's heart is a missionary heart and the hearts of Christians need to be like his. In the light of all of this, there can be no doubt that God wanted (and still wants) the message of salvation spread to all nations through his chosen people. The Old Testament sets forth the missionary purpose of God. The church needs to be converted to mission!

Dvorak's *New World Symphony* is my favourite piece of classical music. I have listened to it so many times that I sometimes find myself humming it. We need to listen to the mission motif in God's Word so that it becomes a familiar tune that touches our hearts. We cannot allow mission to be marginalised in our churches. It must be kept central. Mission must be returned to its rightful place at the heart of the church. Martin Goldsmith speaks of the situation like this:

> ...mission appears to be an optional extra to be indulged in by those who are spiritually keen and who happen to be interested in it. Furthermore, those who try to stimulate a belief that world mission is an integral part of the life of the church find that such exhortations fail to make much impact.[2]

Trevor Harris has put his finger on the problem: "...part of the problem is that our churches are failing to teach worldwide mission as a basic theme of the whole Bible."[3] A church should not become inward looking.

---

[2] Cited in *The Great Omission* by Trevor Harris, Evangelical Press, 2005, p.17.

[3] Trevor Harris, *The Great Omission*, Evangelical Press, 2005, p.17.

But in reality the self-centred ethos that pervades society is becoming increasingly prevalent in the church. Harris points out that a genuine concern for mission is based on a deep sense of personal indebtedness to Christ and an appreciation of the great cost of our redemption.[4]

All people are created in the image of God. This image is reflected clearer (or ought to be) in those who are called Christians. This image is not only reflected in who we are, but also in what we do. As such, those who are called by his name are to seek to accomplish his purpose and to serve his mission. Christopher Wright says: "I wanted them to see not just that the Bible contains a number of texts which happen to provide a rationale for missionary endeavours but that the whole Bible is itself a missional phenomenon."[5] He points out that from the opening accounts in Genesis, God is revealed as one who seeks relationship with his creation.[6] Thus, after the fall of man into sin, the stage is set for the rest of the Bible to describe and recount God's single-minded purpose to reconcile his creation to himself. This is a crucial spiritual perspective.[7]

The mission of God is clearly expressed in the call of Abraham recorded in Genesis chapter twelve. While God's words of promise certainly include rich blessings for him and his family, the key to understanding their missional significance lies in the purpose clauses. God's promise was given, "so that" (Gen. 12:2) all the people of the earth would be blessed.[8] Israel was to be God's missionary people to the rest of the world and that plan is still being rolled out.

The incarnation literally embodies the heart of God for mankind and is the missionary model for reaching the world with the gospel. Christ's ministry was missional and focused on establishing the kingdom of God:

---

[4] *Ibid.*

[5] Christopher Wright, *The Mission of God*, Downers Grove: InterVarsity Press, 2006, 32.

[6] *Ibid.*, 54.

[7] *Ibid.*, 55.

[8] Walter Kaiser, Israel's Missionary Call', *Perspectives on the World Christian Movement*, 12.

It is the glory of God's kingdom being launched on earth as in heaven, generating a new state of affairs in which the power of evil has been decisively defeated, the new creation has been decisively launched, and Jesus' followers have been commissioned and equipped to put that victory and that inaugurated new world into practice.[9]

We are ambassadors for Christ. One author has said, "We cannot be ambassadors for a kingdom that does not have our full allegiance"[10] Christians must have a missional perspective and be the people God intends them to be. Robert Coleman expresses it like this:

Christian disciples are sent, men and women—sent out in the same work and world evangelism to which the Lord was sent, and for which He gave His life. Evangelism is not an optional accessory to our life. It is the heartbeat of all that we are called to be and do. It is the commission of the church which gives meaning to all else that is undertaken in the name of Christ. With this purpose clearly in focus, everything which is done and said has the glorious fulfilment in God's redemptive purpose.[11]

John Piper points out that the goal of mission is to bring people into the worship of God and sees mission as a natural outcome of worship. He says, "Missions begins and ends in worship"[12] The church exists to worship God, to fellowship with God's people, to disciple believers, to minister to the needs of those in the church and last (but not least) to engage in evangelism.

Ministering to the needs of its members is essential to a church's health and survival. This does not mean that all activity should be focused on caring for its own membership. We must go beyond the maintenance mode and be intentionally missional. Mission is essentially a work of the

---

[9] Tom Wright, *Surprised by Hope*, New York: Harper Collins Publishers, 2008, 204.

[10] Ed Stetzer and Philip Nation, *Compelled by Love*, Birmingham: New Hope Publishers, 2008, 26.

[11] Robert Coleman, 'The Master Plan', *Perspectives on the World Christian Movement*, 125.

[12] John Piper, 'Let the Nations Be Glad', *Perspectives on the World Christian Movement*, 64.

Holy Spirit and he is the Spirit of truth and holiness and will not be involved in activity that is untrue or unholy.

Today's cultural setting bears similarities with that of the early church. Christ ministered at a time when institutional religion had virtually collapsed. The legalistic rituals of the Pharisees created a dead spiritual environment but there was a surge in spiritual interest and many were searching for God.

The problem with the church abstaining from involvement in social issues is that it does not help to bridge the credibility gap between the church and the world.

## Identifying the Way Forward

Political parties produce manifestos. In these ambitious documents, they publish their aspirations and policies. An understanding of their position and purpose may be gleaned from their manifestos. Such documents usually contain promises whereby political parties inform the public what they will do if elected. These statements spell out their intentions and the course of action they will adopt if or when elected to government. So the manifesto sets out the agenda for the future direction. It states what the party (or individual or independent candidate) wants to achieve and how they intend to go about it. In the *Communist Manifesto* (1848), Karl Marx and Friedrich Engels, social scientists, authors and political theorists, developed a philosophy known as communist theory. The *Communist Manifesto* set out a plan that proposed that the capitalist system of private ownership would be replaced by a communist society in which capital would be communally owned. It shaped the vision of communism as a movement. As such, it was a seminal and influential document. Karl Marx called religion "the opium of the masses." What he meant is generally misunderstood. It was not religion *per se* he was talking about, rather he was referring to the kind of religion that fails to address social issues. It was a stinging but justifiable criticism, aimed at those who professed faith in Christ but did not speak out against the oppression of the weak by the powerful.

When Jesus stood up to read the Scriptures in the synagogue at Nazareth, he read words from the Old Testament book of Isaiah:

> The Spirit of the Lord is upon Me,
> Because He has anointed Me
> To preach the gospel to the poor;
> He has sent Me to heal the broken-hearted,
> To proclaim liberty to the captives
> And recovery of sight to the blind,
> To set at liberty those who are oppressed;
> To proclaim the acceptable year of the Lord.
>
> (Luke 4:18-19)

He then sat down to teach, as was the custom. These words are known as "The Nazareth Manifesto." They are a public statement setting the agenda for his ministry. Jesus came to his hometown of Nazareth and to the synagogue to great acclaim. People were amazed, "All...marvelled at the gracious words which proceeded out of His mouth" (Luke 4:22). But the story of Jesus returning to his hometown is instructive. The warmth of the welcome he received soon turned to anger. Jesus becomes an object of hate and focus of the people's rage. What was it that turned the people against Jesus and so very quickly? Why did they so decisively reject the prophet whom they had so enthusiastically welcomed? It is in this very passage of Scripture that Jesus said, "no prophet is accepted in his own country" (v.24). The church has a prophetic ministry, to speak and act as God wants. But there is resentment of and resistance to this kind of message. For Christ on that occasion the outcome was quite sinister because the people to whom he was speaking, namely the devout adherents of the religious establishment, tried to kill him.

What did he say that was so offensive? The mood changed when Jesus began to tell them that God loved those outside their own religious community. In their thinking, they had reduced God to a local, tribal deity who doted on them alone. The people loved Jesus until he started to talk about how God loved foreigners too. The thought that God's favour could be extended in this way was offensive to them. They were privileged citizens and they were not going to share the rights of citizenship with outsiders. Perhaps the wealthy loved Jesus until he started to talk about loving the poor because that would cost more than they were willing to pay. The difficulty comes when Jesus challenges us to reach out to those on the edge. This stretches our thinking and our emotional and financial resources. That kind of preaching is uncomfortable to those who do not want to look beyond the boundaries of their own community and self interest.

But the Spirit of the Lord desires to operate through the church in establishing and extending the kingdom of God. So we must do all that we can to keep mission central to church life. The way forward begins by knowing what mission is all about. A necessary first step, therefore, is helping people to understand that mission is more than evangelism. Unpacking that might mean helping people to unlearn what they have received (or assumed) and labelled and dismissed as the "social gospel."

## What Is Mission?

The church's mission is rooted in the *Missio Dei*, that is, the calling of Israel to be a light to all nations: "I will make you as a light for the nations, that my salvation may reach to the end of the earth." (Isa. 49:6).[13] Christ's commission to his disciples says that they were to be his witnesses to the ends of the earth and the end of time (Matt. 28:18-20; Acts 1:8). Mission expresses the biblical idea of being sent. This is conveyed in the words of Jesus, "As the Father has sent me, I am sending you" (John 20:21). Eric Wright offers a helpful definition of mission:

> By mission I mean the total calling of the church as it reflects the eternal purpose of God. This involves an upward activity—worship, thanksgiving, intercession, fellowship with God. It also involves an inward aspect—the organisation of individual believers into local churches, their edification or discipling, their care and comfort, their mutual fellowship and training. Finally, it involves an outward activity—witnessing or evangelism, concern and care for the needs of the community, and particularly missionary outreach, a commitment of the resources necessary to plant churches among the unreached in the community and among all the peoples of the earth.[14]

---

[13] For a fuller explanation of *Missio Dei* see L. Pachauau, '*Missio Dei*' in John Corrie (ed.), *Dictionary of Mission Theology: Evangelical Foundations*, Northampton: England: IVP, 2007, pp.232-234.

[14] Eric E. Wright, *A Practical Theology of Missions: Dispelling the Mystery; Recovering the Passion*, Day One, Leominster: England, 2010, p.18.

Though evangelism is central to mission, mission is more than evangelism. Evangelism is about proclaiming the gospel message and inviting people to believe in Christ for salvation. Mission is a broader term that incorporates the idea of Christian social responsibility. Christians need to co-operate in prayer, planning and participation in the evangelisation of the whole world. That work will necessitate a holistic approach to the spiritual, physical and psychological needs of people struggling to survive in adverse political, social, economic and environmental conditions.

Some Christians want to define mission as evangelism because this is their limited theological understanding of mission.[15] Others are in situations that are geared towards evangelism and change is just too much to think about. Many feel that evangelism will be diluted in a wider mission agenda. Largely, in the West (though not exclusively so), the evangelical church, which is oriented towards evangelism and mission in broader terms, is just too daunting to contemplate. It is difficult to get these kinds of churches to consider mission because as far as they are concerned their members already have enough commitments in attending church on Sundays, the mid-week prayer meeting and Bible study, teaching at Sunday school, leading worship, preaching and outreach (usually defined as sharing the message of the gospel and distributing literature that shows the way of salvation). This is essential and vital work and must be continued but it must not be *either* evangelism *or* mission rather it must be mission with evangelism at its core. There are a number of dimensions to missiology.[16]

First and foremost, mission must bear witness to the truth of the gospel "that Christ Jesus came into the world to save sinners" (1 Tim.

---

[15] I am referring here to those who understand the church's mission as proclaiming the gospel message and inviting people to believe in Christ for salvation. It is acknowledged that evangelism can be defined in broader terms such as the Luasanne Covenant and the Manila Manifesto.

[16] See J. A. Kirk, 'Missiology', in Sinclair Ferguson and David F Wright (eds.), *New Dictionary of Theology*, Leicester: England: IVP, 1988 (reprint, 1994) pp.434-436.

1:15). This is an apostolic gospel that is doctrinally defined by Scripture, to lead people to faith and wholeness in Christ. This will involve evangelism, including a reasoned defence of the faith (apologetics) and pre-evangelism. Pre-evangelism is about removing obstacles that hinder the proclamation of the gospel. A farmer does not plough a field that is full of boulders. These objects must be removed prior to ploughing and planting seed. Bearing witness to the truth as it is in Christ is both verbal and visual. There is a message to be proclaimed; a message that can be *heard* but there is also a necessity to live in such a way, as individuals and as a community of believers, so as to make it possible for this message to be *seen* as it is lived out in the transformed lives of redeemed people living in harmonious relationship.

This involves demonstrating what it means to be a redeemed, transformed and transformative community. In a sense, it is not only about *doing* mission but *being* mission. Mission is not the *raison d'être* of the church. But the church is a community that bears witness to God's glorious grace made manifest in a new order. Mission, in this sense, demonstrates what it means in practice to be a people of integrity, peace and hope in a world that is corrupt, distressed and despairing. Part of the church's mission is to bear testimony to the practical reality of God's unmerited grace by being a people who exercise forgiveness and looking out for the needs of others in the family of God by sharing the resources God has given. The church must work towards the elimination of prejudice and suspicion within its own multi-ethnic communities before it can expect to be heard on this matter by others outside its precincts. In a postmodern age, the church must exercise influence not as a domineering or controlling power but rather as a servant. In this way, the church is to be both a sign and an agent of God's purposes.

This brings us to the second dimension of mission, namely the church's role as a servant. Mission must be motivated by genuine compassion. The church must not engage in aiding others only as a means to a greater end. Mission must have no ulterior motive. The church has a role to play in working in development programmes with victims of natural catastrophes (drought, flood, famine) and the consequent diseases associated with such phenomena.[17] The church can play an important role in advocating for peaceful solutions to local, national and international conflicts. It can function in the midst of conflict as an agent of practical aid.

Poverty has many forms. It is obviously the lack of food, shelter and clothing. The church's response must address these issues. But poverty is also about lack of opportunity arising out of poor health or poor education. Therefore, mission will include literacy and other educational programmes, particularly health education. This is about addressing disadvantage. Many people in the Third World have no opportunity to go to school for reasons of finance, gender (girls), lack of infrastructure and so on. Many, even in the developed world, drop out because they are facing issues in the home or school environment. Here, there is a need for special programmes to compensate early school leavers for their lack of educational attainment.

Mission will not neglect those with physical or mental disability. The church also has a particular responsibility to create a society that ministers to the needs of the elderly and the vulnerable. Many people today are suffering from stress, anxiety and depression. Suicides arising out of such feelings are all too frequent, especially among the young. One does not necessarily have to have medical expertise to assist those who are mentally afflicted.[18] There are so many opportunities for service that there is no excuse for a church not being active in mission. Each local church must look to the needs of those in the wider community. Where can it serve? God is close to the broken-hearted (Ps. 34:18) and he wants his people involved in binding up their wounds (Ps. 147:3). Whether it is comforting those who are bereaved, working with children at risk or families in tension, all can be done to the glory of God as mission. There are ministries to rehabilitate offenders against the law, ministries

---

[17] It needs to be asserted that many so-called 'natural disasters' have an all-too human dimension, including floods and famines.

[18] Obviously, professional help is needed for such people and certain mental illnesses can cause some people to be dangerous to themselves and others and great caution is advised.

working with alcoholics, drug addicts and chronic gamblers. This is where the rubber hits the road in terms of mission impacting on society. Mission means reaching out to those who are marginalised, alienated, rejected and despised. The church must minister God's grace to those who need it most.

Thirdly, mission means doing all that can be done to ensure that justice prevails in society. The church has been rightly vocal on many social issues of concern, such as promoting and defending family values. It has been articulate on matters such as divorce, abortion and experimentation on early human life. It has not been silent with regard to sexual issues such as fornication, adultery and homosexuality. It has voiced its objections to pornography and the exploitation of women and children. All of this is good in itself but the church is called upon to do more by way of advocating alternatives to economic policies that are likely to increase homelessness. Many people are badly educated, undernourished and unemployed because of greed and exploitation. A society where racism has not been eradicated is underdeveloped. It may be materially wealthy but it is socially and spiritually poor. Why has the church failed to successfully challenge the inexorable build-up of weapons of mass destruction and the increasing arms trade between rich and poor nations which is contributing to the misery of so many? Frankly, it is because of a failure to realise that there is a social dimension to the gospel. The church is guilty of privatising faith and detaching it from these issues. Vested interests have won out over virtuous interests.

Ensuring that justice prevails in society also involves the equitable distribution of the wealth of material resources so that ordinary people can benefit from their national wealth. Thus mission is about contributing to the creation of a society where material resources are understood as part of God's creation. These resources should not be pillaged and plundered by the elite for the accumulation of vast profits. Sadly not only have Christians stood idly by as this exploitation took place but many have actively participated in it. Why is it left to secular activists to engage in raising conservation awareness and working towards the elimination of pollution when the ultimate ecological ethic is rooted in

God?[19] Mission will necessitate renouncing greed. The church needs to do all that it can to promote a more restrained enjoyment of material goods by all in such a way that future generations will find life sustainable on earth.

## Keeping Mission Central to Church Life

Obviously, no local church can engage in *all* of this kind of activity but each church can engage in *some* aspect of it and in so doing its corporate witness will be greatly enhanced. This catalogue of issues is not meant to overwhelm us with the daunting prospect of tackling all of the world's social ills, rather it indicates the almost inexhaustible opportunity to put matters on the agenda and to get involved in cutting-edge missional activity.

Thus to pray, "Your kingdom come", means preaching the gospel to the poor. To pray, "Your kingdom come", means ministering to the broken-hearted. To pray, "Your kingdom come", means leading those who are spiritual captives to freedom in Christ. To pray, "Your kingdom come", means leading the spiritually blind to behold the Lamb of God who takes away the sin of the world. To pray these words means speaking out on behalf of the oppressed. It means working towards a fairer and more just society. To pray these words is not passive. Prayer of this kind is transformative and it enables those who pray in this manner to continue the work of his kingdom.

The church is called to be prophetic community. Those who work in the cause of the kingdom will encounter the opposition (or at least a lack of sympathy and support) of those who want to protect their own interests. Who has the courage for this sort of mission? Certain sections of the Christian community might well ask if they are fulfilling his mission in this regard. God has invited the church to join him in this great project. As the saying goes, 'familiarity breeds contempt.' Is the Christian community so familiar with this manifesto that it fails to fully realise its radical nature? There are varying degrees of commitment to fulfilling

---

[19] It is acknowledged that there is Christian involvement in environmental issues but what I am arguing here is that it should be a more pervasive element of our ethos.

the details of such a manifesto, which indicate that if there is not contempt for it, then there is complacency about it. God invites the Christian community to play its part in his kingdom enterprise. It needs to make his manifesto its manifesto!

The Nazareth manifesto declares a bias for the poor that the church should never lose sight of. What is good news for the poor if it does not include the alleviation of poverty? The Christian community cannot turn a blind eye to the miserable conditions under which three quarters of the world's population live their lives. To talk about the redistribution of wealth and the sharing of the world's resources and the elimination of poverty not only sounds unattainable but also sounds like communism to Christians who have vested interests in the structural inequalities of the economic world.

There is an obligation not only to dare to imagine a radical alternative but to work towards the achievement of such a reality. The utopian dream may not be achievable but there is a duty to seek to eradicate the dystopian nightmare of those enslaved to poverty and all its attendant social evils. The church should work towards a politics of peace and ethical economics.

Spiritual education must be part of the strategy in keeping mission central to church life. Many Christians are unaware of the reality of poverty in this world and will want to respond when informed. We need to be more diligent in finding ways whereby they can give practical expression to that heartfelt desire. But more fundamentally those engaged in the theological training of ministers have a great responsibility to ensure that they convey the message that "Missionary theology is not an appendix to biblical theology; it belongs at its very core. No doctrine of God, Christ or the Holy Spirit has been expounded completely according to the Bible until it has established the triune God as the God of mission."[20]

It is one of God's communicable attributes that he reaches out to redeem the lost. God is a God of truth and mission is about calling people out of false religion, false philosophy and godless ideologies and 'isms.' God is a God of holiness and mission must bear witness to this by warning

---

[20] George W. Peters, *A Biblical Theology of Missions*, Chicago: Moody, 1972, p.27.

of the final judgement. God is patient and because he is patient judgement is delayed while his mission is being fulfilled. God is a God of goodness and grace, who is "rich in mercy" (Eph. 2:4). Mission must reflect this attribute of God. Because God is love (1 John 4:8, 16) mission will be a loving intervention in the lives of people who need to hear the story of God's love and experience the practical application of that love in acts of kindness and care. God is sovereign and the outworking of his sovereign purposes involves his people engaging in mission. His sovereignty ensures that the outcomes of our missionary endeavours in partnership with him will be in accordance with his will.

God is triune. The Father sent the Son on a mission to redeem the lost. The Son, in turn, sent his disciples to extend and complete the mission he commenced. The Holy Spirit enables and assists in the work of mission by bringing conviction of sin. Engaging in mission is being involved in the fulfilment of God's will. Mission is about the restoration of right relationship with God, which was lost in the Garden of Eden. Christians are privileged ambassadors engaged in this work of reconciliation. Mission is not only intrinsically connected to the person and work of Christ but also to the person and work of the Holy Spirit whose ministry involves executing the decrees of the Father in this world. The incarnation is a missionary event, for Christ came into the world to save sinners. The gospels record the commencement of Christ's missionary activity. The book of Acts documents the continuation of that mission and the book of Revelation emphasises the culmination of that mission.

The names of Christ identify his missionary nature. 'Jesus' means 'Saviour.' 'Emmanuel' emphasises his incarnational missionary journey. 'Master' refers to his missionary message. The "I am" statements of Christ proclaim his missionary purpose: the shepherd, the door, the living water, the bread of life, the way the truth and the life, the resurrection and the life, the light of the world.

God is a communicating God and there is a gospel message to be communicated. Eric Wright says:

> The central activity of missions is the communication of the gospel. Although Christ healed, cast out demons, raised the dead and fed the

hungry, these activities gave way more and more in his second and third years of ministry to teaching. Indeed, the Spirit revealed to John at the beginning of his Gospel that communication was so central to the mission of Christ that one of Christ's most important names is 'Word'. 'In the beginning was the Word, and the Word was with God, and the Word was God.' (John 1:1)...God has been eternally committed to communication and that communication centres on the incarnate Christ.[21]

## Mission Today

Today's world cannot be neatly divided into Christian and non-Christian regions. Certainly, it has to be acknowledged that the '10/40 Window' remains as a challenge to mission. This is a geographical area that refers to regions of the eastern hemisphere located between 10 and 40 degrees north of the equator. It has the highest level of socio-economic challenges and least access to the Christian message and Christian resources on the planet. The '10/40 Window' concept brings into the church's radar an area of the world, with great poverty and lack of access to Christian resources. This area encompasses Saharan and North Africa as well as almost all of Asia. Roughly two-thirds of the world's population live in this region. It is populated by people who are predominantly Muslim, Hindu, Buddhist, Animist, Jewish or Atheist. Many governments in the '10/40 Window' are formally or informally opposed to Christian work of any kind within their borders. Understandably, many Christians want to prioritise mission in this region.

The apostle Paul liked to, "boldly go where no man has gone before." He said: "I make it my ambition to preach the gospel, not where Christ has already been named, lest I build on someone else's foundation, but as it is written, 'Those who have never been told of him will see, and those who have never heard will understand.'" (Rom. 15:20). Such opportunities still exist today but not everybody can avail of them. Not everybody is called to be a 'professional' missionary. Nevertheless, we all have a part to play in mission. From a pastoral point of view keeping mission central to church life is essentially about enabling people to identify areas where they can serve in mission. It is about equipping them

---

[21] Eric E. Wright, *Op. cit.*, p.46.

to fulfil these roles effectively. All believers must be witnesses of the gospel in word and deed. Nobody is exempt from this. People are fearful of participating in mission because they feel under-skilled. Some may be reluctant to be involved in mission because they are ashamed of the gospel and do not want to be associated with, 'that bunch of fundamentalists.' Serious self-examination is required from every believer as a necessary prerequisite to putting mission at the heart of the church.

## Theory and Practice

Former Prime Minister of Ireland, Dr. Garret Fitzgerald, was noted for his great intellect. He is reported to have once said, "That is all very well in *practice* but how does it work out in *theory*?" Whether he actually said this or not I cannot say for certain, but most people are prepared to believe it. All who remember him are amused by the possibility that it could actually be true because he was a theorist. On one occasion, he wore a brown shoe and a black shoe in public. When this was pointed out, he made some feeble excuse about it still being dark when he left home and how he did not want to put on the light which would have disturbed his wife, who was still sleeping. This added to the generally accepted view that he was brilliant but a little out of touch with reality. I wonder if our churches have become like academic academies where learning takes place about mission but evangelism is left to the evangelism team and mission is left to the 'professionals' who occasionally visit our congregations to give power-point presentations, share a brief word from Scripture, tell stories and make subtle financial appeals.

It is easier, in a church context, to arouse interest in mission than it is to stimulate participation in the task of reaching the lost world. Many Christians meditate on and study truth but appear detached from the practical realities of engaging with contemporary culture. Mission is not just a component of the curriculum of Bible colleges and theological seminaries. Mission must be upheld as a core value in the church today. Engaging effectively with our culture will involve a holistic approach to mission because mission involves the whole purpose of God for humanity, including spiritual salvation. This means that Christian mission should encompass issues related to ecology, health, education, social justice (including poverty, race and gender issues) and a host of other issues that intersect with people's lives and concerns.

In every community, there are many people who suffer from depression, stress, anxiety and loneliness. Many people experience suicidal thoughts and sadly for some those thoughts are translated into action, often resulting in their deaths. The church must minister to these people. We must bear testimony to the fact that we are a redeemed and transformed community of people living in harmonious relationship with God and each other. We must offer benevolence, blessing and belonging to people who need help and kindness and meaningful relationship.

The world is a global village and no local church ought to be ignorant of or indifferent to the reality of poverty. It is not enough to say we care. Real compassion acts out the love of God in service and sacrificial giving. The U2 lead singer, Bono, once walked on a stage at a gig and started clapping his hands at three-second intervals. He proclaimed to the audience that "every 3 seconds someone dies of hunger on this planet." A witty reply came back from the crowd: "Then stop clapping your hands, you sadist!" I know some people who were at that event and they felt that Bono was spoiling their party. I wonder if we are like that in the church. Do we resent being presented with statistical data about the reality of poverty? Do we resist the challenge of participating in mission? We are called and commissioned to be partners with God in this project and we need to see it as a privilege and an exciting adventure.

## Global Village[22]

Here is a peek into the disturbing reality that we find so uncomfortable. If you could fit the entire population of the world into a village consisting of a hundred people, maintaining the proportions of all the people living on Earth, that village would consist of 57 Asians, 21 Europeans, 14 Americans (North, Central and South) and 8 Africans. There would be 52 women and 48 men. It would be comprised of 30 Caucasians and 70 non-Caucasians. There would be 30 'Christians' (many of whom would be nominal Christians) and 70 people of other faiths. There would be

---

[22] See *http://www.100people.org/statistics_100stats.php*

89 heterosexuals and 11 homosexuals. Would it surprise you to know that six people would possess 59 per cent of the wealth? They would all come from the USA. In this global village, which depicts the reality of world poverty, 80 people out of the hundred would live in poverty. Seventy would be illiterate. Fifty would suffer from hunger. One would be dying and one being born. Only one person would own a computer. Only one person would have a university degree. Looking at the world like this helps us understand the reality of poverty.

But consider the following: If you woke up this morning in good health, you are better off than one million people who won't live through the week. If you have never experienced the horror of war, the anguish of prison, the pain of torture or been close to death from starvation, then you are better off than 500 million people! If you can go to your place of worship without fear that someone will assault or kill you, then you are more privileged than 3 billion (that's right) people. If you have food in your fridge, clothes on your back, a roof over your head and a place to sleep, you are wealthier than 75 per cent of the world's population. If you currently have money in the bank or in your wallet or a few coins in your purse, you are one of eight of the privileged few in the world. If your parents are still alive and still married, you are a rare individual.[23]

Such daunting challenges can immobilise us or inspire us. So we need a universal vision but with a particular focus. Nevertheless, the question must be asked: What are we doing about it? If the answer to that question is 'nothing', we are in serious trouble as individuals and as churches. Listen to what Jesus has to say about this:

> When the Son of Man comes in his glory, and all the angels with him, then he will sit on his glorious throne. Before him will be gathered all the nations, and he will separate people one from another as a shepherd separates the sheep from the goats. And he will place the sheep on his right, but the goats on the left. Then the King will say to those on his right, 'Come, you who are blessed by my Father, inherit the kingdom prepared for you from the foundation of the world. For I was hungry and you gave me food, I was thirsty and you gave me drink, I was a stranger and you welcomed me,

---

[23] Since you are reading this book, it means you are not one of the 2 billion people who cannot read.

I was naked and you clothed me, I was sick and you visited me, I was in prison and you came to me.' Then the righteous will answer him, saying, 'Lord, when did we see you hungry and feed you, or thirsty and give you drink? And when did we see you a stranger and welcome you, or naked and clothe you? And when did we see you sick or in prison and visit you?' And the King will answer them, 'Truly, I say to you, as you did it to one of the least of these my brothers, you did it to me.' 'Then he will say to those on his left, 'Depart from me, you cursed, into the eternal fire prepared for the devil and his angels. For I was hungry and you gave me no food, I was thirsty and you gave me no drink, I was a stranger and you did not welcome me, naked and you did not clothe me, sick and in prison and you did not visit me.' Then they also will answer, saying, 'Lord, when did we see you hungry or thirsty or a stranger or naked or sick or in prison, and did not minister to you?' Then he will answer them, saying, 'Truly, I say to you, as you did not do it to one of the least of these, you did not do it to me.' And these will go away into eternal punishment, but the righteous into eternal life.'

Frequently, when we partake of the Lord's Supper, we read or recite a passage of Scripture from Paul's first letter to the Corinthians:

> ...the Lord Jesus on the night when he was betrayed took bread, and when he had given thanks, he broke it, and said, "This is my body which is for you. Do this in remembrance of me." In the same way also he took the cup, after supper, saying, 'This cup is the new covenant in my blood. Do this, as often as you drink it, in remembrance of me.' For as often as you eat this bread and drink the cup, you proclaim the Lord's death until he comes. Whoever, therefore, eats the bread or drinks the cup of the Lord in an unworthy manner will be guilty concerning the body and blood of the Lord. Let a person examine himself, then, and so eat of the bread and drink of the cup. (1 Cor. 11:23-32)

We use this to remind ourselves of our security in Christ and to celebrate the New Covenant. We use it to see what we are doing that is wrong. But there are sins of *omission* as well as *commission* and failing to do good things is sin: "So whoever knows the right thing to do and fails to do it, for him it is sin" (Jas. 4:17). What would happen if we were to read the passage from Matthew 25 (cited above) at the Lord's Table as an aid to self-examination in the light of Scripture? Probably, some well-meaning soul would try to offer an antidote to the 'guilt-trip' by saying, 'There is therefore now no condemnation for those who are in Christ Jesus' (Rom.

8:1). There would probably be a sigh of relief from all those who feel that this lets them off the hook. But that verse from Romans does not excuse our apathy in a world of inequalities and injustices and suffering and greed. Christ is saying that his true disciples will be those who care for the destitute. Not just care *about* them but actually *provide* practical care. The fruit of true discipleship will be evident in practical ways. How concerned are we really about people's physical well-being?

Furthermore, how concerned are we about the eternal destiny of those in our world, especially those in our immediate community? There is a story about parents who overheard their five-year-old daughter, Sarah, telling her little friend about Jesus. Sarah told her friend that if she believed in Jesus and prayed, he would forgive her sins and she would go to heaven. The little girl was convinced and prayed and then asked, "Will my mommy go to heaven too?" Sarah replied, "Yea, if she believes in Jesus, but if you don't want her there don't tell her about Jesus!" I have no doubt that if you tell this story to a group of Christians they will enjoy the humour. But it begs the question: Are we telling people about Jesus?

The best way to keep mission central to the life of the church is for the leadership to get in tune with the rhythm of God's heartbeat and to facilitate opportunities for church members to engage in mission. Mission is the metronome (the device ticking at a selected rate to mark time for musicians) that helps us measure the pace of progress in God's purposes. In conducting the affairs of the church, we must employ diverse gifting to engage harmoniously in producing the majestic melody of mission to the glory of God.

*Chapter 4*

# Reading the Bible for Inclusive Justice

## *Monica Melanchthon*

**What Is Mission?**

Mission can no longer be visualised as a kind of 'spiritual warfare' in which missionaries fight battles to conquer other religions and to occupy other people's conscience in order to Christianise the world. Such positions are fast losing their appeal, regardless of the agencies that endorse comprehensive or far-reaching plans for missionary world occupation. Christians are now confronted with the dilemma of how to root non-colonial and imperialistic understandings of mission in Christian faith and tradition for political, social and theological reasons.

I am personally drawn to a position offered by Theodore Ahrens on Matthew 6:10 "Your kingdom come, your will be done on earth as it is in heaven." He sees this as the *magna carta* of Christian mission, offering a perspective on mission that is true to the Gospel and yet not imperialistic.[1]

---

[1] In *Quest for Justice: Perspectives on Mission and Unity*, George Matthew Nalunnakkal and Abraham P. Athyal (eds.), New Delhi/Nagpur/Chennai: ISPCK/NCCI/Gurukul, 2000.

He says that the prayer says many things:

- It presupposes that what is happening presently on earth does not correspond well with the will or wishes of God and so it is a critique of what the world is today. It is a critique of and a protest against all the dehumanising systems and structures of this world, which need to be dismantled for the purposes of wholistic life for all, a signifying feature of the reign of God.

- It is an expression of hope, a prayer that looks forward to the merger between heaven and earth into one sphere wherein the will of God—creator, redeemer and sanctifier—will be fulfilled. So, the reign of God is not a human possibility alone. It is not quite here yet and, at the same time, it is here. It becomes manifest in the act of people joining Jesus in saying this prayer, which Jesus taught his friends. It is the expression of a radical hope that through the mission of Jesus Christ, through the sharing of the Good News, a life lived in the Spirit of Christ was, is and will continue to be a real and wholesome possibility for anyone anywhere in the world. Cynicism, religious fundamentalism, destruction, violence and corruption, or in short evil—they have their place in our times. But so does God's will, which shall also find its place in our time for eternity.

- It is a radical call to commit oneself to the will of God. It is an imperative issued to people to join Jesus in doing what Jesus did during his lifetime on earth and thereby bring in the reign of God. All those who say this prayer are to or should take a position with Jesus in his mission of faith and love against the harsh realities of evil, violence, destruction and discrimination. The prayer is therefore at once a prayer, a protest and an expression of faith and hope.

It is hoped that people who say this prayer for the coming of the Kingdom of God will respect what others believe in or worship or live for. They will listen to them in order to understand them and hear what they hear and see what they see. Christians in mission need to respect that people with variant beliefs also live with commitments of their own and long to live lives of justice. Some are motivated by their identities, others by their conscience. Still others are driven by their notions of the divine and the messages they receive from there. Most have a sense of mission and Christian mission takes place and takes shape amid other missions of justice that others pursue.[2]

Christians who do not betray their faith nor deride the missions of others will find themselves constantly challenged to go back to their own roots and to re-examine afresh their understandings of mission. As Christians enter into such self-critical exercise, their lives will gain some missionary credibility and churches will become vibrant places. Christian mission is therefore about freedom—it is the endeavor to risk a life in the Spirit of Christ. Faith in God and love for one another, the so-called vertical and horizontal, cannot and should not compete. In faith, we trust that the ingredients that make for a life in the Spirit of Christ (e.g. love for one another, forgiveness, confidence, joy and encouragements), though mediated through our words and bodies, are gifts from God. Faithfully, we expect such gifts to come from God—in pure gratitude.

Such faith will open our eyes to anything that may threaten the body, the freedom, the dignity, the future of others. Faith will motivate and help people to try and work within the framework of contextual structures to the best of their abilities in a spirit of love and service. Faith will let love govern our concern for the world and while testing the potential love as a motivating force we learn the need of faith in God. We learn anew to pray: "Your kingdom come, your will be done." Love needs faith and faith needs the practice of love to test the sustaining power of God in the reality of our lives.

It is essential that we utilise our faith and love for the realisation of justice and wholistic life for all, for the eradication of inequities and imbalances in society and for the ushering in of the reign of God. But for one to recognise this as mission one needs to be able to derive this also within the biblical text, a source of God's revelation. I argue that this is made possible only through inclusive biblical interpretation—a method of reading and interpreting that takes cognizance of multiple voices and subdued voices both within the text and within the faith community, voices heretofore undermined or rejected or ignored. I am convinced

---

[2] *Ibid.*

that the manner in which one approaches the Bible and interprets it influences the way in which mission is understood.

## My Experience

I offer this as an introductory remark and premise upon which I build the rest of my paper.

In the recent past, I have done bible studies and preached on texts such as the story of Bathsheba in 2 Samuel 11, experience of Miriam in Numbers chapter 12, the story of Lot's daughters in Genesis 19, the book of the Song of Songs and the song of Mary in Luke 4, to name just a few. As a woman interpreter of the Bible, I tend to lean towards texts relating to women characters. My intention in reading these stories, particularly those from the Old Testament, is to call attention to texts that are often left out of our lectionaries or ignored by the average reader of the Bible. The reasons may be many—ranging from the disturbing questions these texts raise to the notion that these texts have no relevance. But my goal was to stir them into seeing with their prior knowledge of who God is and what God is doing in the world that can help them evaluate biblical texts considered problematic or irrelevant. As a theological educator, I am often left feeling frustrated and a little sad, because the exercise is a failure in the case of most students. For many this is the "Word of God" and if it seems to say it is okay to humiliate a woman, or to oppress a slave, then it is okay to do so. I therefore wonder:

- Why are people not able to respond adequately to issues of justice?

- If one does not see how one is himself or herself a possible victim or perpetrator of injustice, how does or can one see another victim of injustice?

- What is it that hinders one from seeing injustice in the world and responding to it?

I had wrongly assumed that most men who claim sensitivity to issues of women or women by virtue of being women and their commitment to issues of justice, with a strong sense of mission and ministry and service, would have different perspectives on these texts about women, rape, incest, sexuality, love and justice. It was either their notion of 'biblical authority' that took precedence over their own particularities or perhaps a stubbornness to change since there was much at stake for them personally. I have since reflected on this, wondering about and pondering over why there is so much resistance to gender justice or equality in society between caste groups or the like, and realised that the lack of self-awareness and their commitment to the Bible are often related. While leading discussions on biblical texts, I have noted that a few of them—male or female—have never thought about what a woman might think about some of these texts, or a person who is victim of oppression and marginalisation. Laws such as the one found in Exodus 22:16-17, which considers the rape of an unmarried female as an insult to her father rather than as violence to the female herself, or the law in Deut. 22:28-29, which requires an unmarried rape victim to marry her rapist, show little consideration to the female victim. How might a raped woman feel about marrying her rapist? An Indian would probably understand the cultural and historical reasons why such a law may have been necessary because it would be quite difficult to find a marriage partner for a raped woman. Even so, the law, a part of the religious tradition, disregards the needs and the experiences of the woman.

My point, more generally, is that the current exclusions within the church tradition and society reflect these exclusions within biblical law or negative portrayals of women and other marginalised groups in the biblical text. They match and contribute to negative portrayals and treatment of women in church and society. Such texts have implications for women seeking ordination or a more active role within the church. The impact of such positions is that the gifts women have for ministry are devalued and the great contributions that women have made historically to the life of the church are ignored. Ultimately, these traditions of the church do not take into account the perspectives of or their consequences for women.

Women are not the only group to be devalued in this way. A failure to consider the realities of other groups, such as *Adivasis*, dalits, HIV and AIDS sufferer and affected, the differently abled, those of different sexual orientation, the poor, the foreigner and the violated, is discernible. Whether we recognise it or not, the biblical text and its underlying values shape how we think of our lives of faith and the issues of the contemporary Christian community.

To realise inclusive justice, we need to engage in biblical interpretation that is inclusive. We should aim to arrive at interpretations that are inclusive, that are liberative for all, but this is possible only if we utilise methods and hermeneutical categories that include the voices, the experiences and the reflections of the community, of those who have been heretofore ignored or left out of the task of biblical interpretation. These are women, children and the marginalised for political or social reasons. Our effort to determine and understand what mission is needs to be inclusive of these voices. This requires further thought on the issues of biblical authority, our teaching styles, i.e., the manner in which we communicate the truths of the Bible, who is included and excluded in the exercise of bible reading and interpreting and clarify our theological and hermeneutical bases for biblical interpretation.

### Discerning our Mission—A Community Endeavour

The Bible is central to our Christian identity and self-understanding, life and praxis and it remains a permanent source of authority, faith and inspiration for determining the mission of the church. Yet the ways in which we use the Bible is deeply contested, and there is little agreement on the nature of biblical authority and the principles of biblical interpretation.[3] While we need to affirm the richness and diversity of the Bible and the many traditions of interpretation, we should struggle to come to a new understanding of how to make better use of the Bible in and for mission.

Ours is a context in which biblical interpretations do matter; they do shape our world. As the Indian context constantly reminds us, biblical interpretations have life and death consequences; they shape the response the church and the ordinary person make to social realities. Our interpretations and understandings of the biblical text therefore have effects. The Bible is a significant text in the history of those of us who

---

[3] Ivy George, "From Proclamation to Presence: Toward an Asian Hermeneutic of Christian Mission," *JAAT* 2, no. 1 (1997) 78-94.

have accepted it as Scripture. The history of the Bible in India and its reception remains complex and ambiguous. In many ways, the Bible has been of service to both the oppressor and the liberator; it has sustained the caste system, the discrimination of women and negative attitudes to people of diverse faiths and struggled against it. But the Bible is also a symbol of the presence of the God of life with the church and a resource in her struggle for survival, liberation and life.

There are many scriptural texts on mission and they need to be viewed more comprehensively and not reduced simply to the Great Commission.[4] Those who work on discovering the biblical foundations of mission should also pay heed to the insights offered by contemporary hermeneutics, namely cross-textual, relational, liberation, inculturation and postmodern hermeneutics. Such an endeavor will be possible only by scholars, those that are socially engaged or also called 'organic intellectuals' immersed and familiar with the needs and aspirations of the community of which they are a part. This requires collaboration between readers of the Bible in the academy and readers of the Bible in poor and marginalised communities, by those in the pews, where the Bible is a significant text. The biblical scholar has to be critical in his or her listening to the interpretations of the poor and marginalised.[5] The objective of such an exercise is of course to identify the content of Christian mission, along with the community, including the people on the periphery of society so that they too will find their freedom to religious self-determination.

In the context of religious and cultural plurality, it may be even beneficial for the church to allow our neighbours to read the relevant passages and interpret to us the spiritual meaning of texts. Such an exercise, whether with the neighbour or the community, might contribute to the deconstruction of traditional views on mission and enable us to

---

[4] There are many recent articles that have very convincingly argued that the Great Commission is in some ways a text of terror for all people who do not share the Eurocentric ideology of Christian triumphalism.

[5] Gerald O. West, *The Academy of the Poor: Towards a Dialogical Reading of the Bible*, Sheffield: Sheffield Academic Press, 1999, 49.

appreciate the spiritual depths of the Christian scriptures seen through the eyes of the poor and the neighbor. Equipping the people of God with skills to derive appropriate and meaningful interpretations of the biblical text, interpretations that are in line with the values of the Gospel, that enable the ushering in of the kingdom of God and that foster the doing of God's will on earth, is also the mission of the church.

## Discerning the Word of God in Community

The issue of 'authority' is a complex issue in the Indian church. Why is the Bible authoritative? How is it authoritative? These are questions that have not been sufficiently dealt with in the Indian context. For most people, it the "Word of God" but what this means and how does it become the word of God is again a contested issue. The 'Word of God' is not found in the letter of Scripture. It is us, human beings, who determine what constitutes Scripture.[6] Thus the meaning of scripture—the 'Word of God'—can only be apprehended within the context of the "living spirit of the living community," (Boff) the church. It becomes the Word in the ongoing relationship between community and scripture. A critical and liberative approach to biblical interpretation defines authority as partnership, where the voice of God emerges from Scripture in the context of dialogue within faith communities.[7] This Scripture is neither absolute, nor ahistorical. It is definitely not neutral, for "it reflects to different degrees the relations and structures of race, gender and class which empower some persons and disenfranchise others."[8]

The 'Word' is revealed through a canonised text and yet this revelation is not confined to a single era or a single interpretation of Scripture. This is made evident by the fact that the Bible offers and makes possible multiple readings in varied historical periods and in multiple

---

[6] Letty M. Russell, "Authority and the Challenge of Feminist Interpretation," in Letty M. Russell *(ed.), Feminist Interpretation of the Bible,* Philadelphia: Westminster Press, 1985, 137-46.

[7] Phyllis A Bird, "The Authority of the Bible," in *The New Interpreter's Bible,* vol. 1, Nashville, Tennessee: Abingdon Press, 1994, 33-64.

[8] W. Randolph Tate, *Interpreting the Bible: A Handbook of Terms and Methods,* Peabody, MA: Hendrickson, 2006, 174.

cultural contexts. So, when I read the Bible, I do so with the belief that it is a dynamic text; the 'Living word,' the "word made flesh," which *dwelt* amongst us and I must be continually open to new revelation whether it comes from a dalit woman, a child or an HIV sufferer. This is not to say that I am not rooted in my faith. There are some things that I am absolutely certain about—the non-negotiable rule, which is the imperative to fight against discrimination, cruelty, violence in any and all its forms, and the importance of love, faith, hope, charity, humility, justice and grace. The 'Word of God' can only be heard as a Living word by engaging creatively with this din of voices from very different political contexts, voices searching for freedom, equality, justice and well-being in times of violence and empire. Such a radical democratic understanding of the Bible requires an equally far-reaching democratising of biblical interpretation.

But the text is by no means wide open, subject to any interpretation by the reader. Interpretation is always "innovative, more or less arbitrary, and always personal, but certainly not without limits or constraints" (Boff). We as readers need to establish boundaries of meaning beyond which interpretation cannot proceed. The community determines the criteria for setting the boundaries, criteria such as the Gospel of Jesus Christ—justice, equality, freedom, dignity, peace and reconciliation. So, a renewed understanding of the nature and function of scripture and the notion of the "Word of God" is essential for an inclusive interpretation of the text.

## Enabling the Community to Become Critical Readers and Interpreters

It is essential that the biblical reader is made conscious of the values of hierarchical systems both in the text and in the world around them, which have been subsequently internalised. The educational models that we follow in the church in India is akin to the banking style, denying our students the opportunity for creativity and insight that would enable them to recognise the systems that disadvantage them[9] and transform them.

---

[9] Paulo Friere, *The Pedagogy of the Oppressed*, Thirtieth Anniversary Edition, trans. Myra Bergman Ramos, New York: Continuum, 2003, 72.

We see our students as storehouses where we might deposit our readings and interpretations of the biblical text, or treat them as passive recipients, thereby hindering them from developing a critical consciousness to analyse the world and the text and to intervene in that world to transform it—to get rid of its inequities.[10]

### Need for Inclusive Biblical Interpretation

A critical approach to biblical interpretation requires that a biblical text is evaluated before it is accepted and obeyed. This evaluation entails assessing its underlying and embedded ideologies in the text. In simple terms, "ideology" refers to a dominant value system in a society that people take for granted even though it serves the interests of the powerful at the expense of the less powerful. For example, patriarchy, a system that privileges men over women, is an ideology, and feminist biblical scholars have struggled for decades to unmask the patriarchal nature of biblical texts. As one feminist scholar wrote many years ago:

> Not only is scripture interpreted by a long line of men and proclaimed in patriarchal churches, it is also authored by men, written in androcentric language, reflective of religious male experience, selected and transmitted by male religious leadership. Without question, the Bible is a male book.[11]

Unfortunately, women readers of biblical texts have appropriated and learned to identify with that male perspective and read texts that are contrary to their own interests. Most people often read the Bible in a way that is counter to their own spiritual, emotional and physical health and well-being. Just as women have become more aware of male ideological interests in biblical texts in recent years, additional groups have identified other patterns of dominance and subordination in the biblical text based on race, caste, religion, former colonised nation status and so forth.

---

[10] *Ibid.*, 73.

[11] Elisabeth Schussler Fiorenza, "The Will to Choose or to Reject: Continuing Our Critical Work," in Letty M. Russell (ed.), *Feminist Interpretation of the Bible*, Philadelphia: Westminster Press, 1985, 130.

In addition, if we understand mission to be the realisation of justice that is inclusive, then our approach to reading and interpreting the biblical text also needs to be just, that is, inclusive of persons and insights that are usually rejected or ignored. Inclusion, according to Eric Law, requires a commitment to "extending our boundary" and takes into consideration "another's needs, interests, experience, and perspective, which will lead to a clearer understanding of ourselves and others, fuller description of the issue at hand, and possibly a new negotiated boundary of the community to which we belong."[12] In other words, a critical and inclusive approach recognises the value of engaging the realities of those who have traditionally been subjugated and sidelined. By doing so, however, new issues are raised about biblical texts themselves as a moral resource. Hearing the witness of women, the dalit or *adivasi*, the tribal and the person living with HIV and AIDS should force us to question the subordination of women and the acceptance of abuse against them, among other things, in biblical texts. Bruce Birch cautions us to remember that "Israel's story is not intended to model normative behaviour in all its particulars."[13]

> Thus, for example, the Old Testament reflects in much of its testimony, a subordinate view of women that is not in harmony with the broader vision of love, justice, and wholeness made clear throughout the Old Testament. This broader vision itself roots in God's activity and will, and the church must claim and apply that vision to issues of the subordination of women in ways that go beyond what the biblical community could have imagined.[14]

## Theological Basis for an Inclusive Approach to Scripture

Being open to inclusion will result in sensitive and perhaps hard questions being raised about which biblical elements must be retrieved and those that must be reclaimed—and those are not easy questions to answer. So

---

[12] Eric H. F. Law, *Inclusion: Making Room for Grace*, St. Louis, MO: Chalice, 2000, 42.

[13] Bruce C. Birch, *Let Justice Roll Down: The Old Testament, Ethics and Christian Life*, Louisville, Kentucky: Westminster/John Knox Press, 1991, 43.

[14] *Ibid.*

we require a clear theological basis for a critical and inclusive approach to biblical interpretation. It depends on two basic theological positions or questions: How we perceive the Bible and how we perceive God? Engendering a critical approach to the Bible requires us to acknowledge that the Bible is a human witness to God's interventions in the world during a particular period of time; and though it reveals to us the "Word of God", it is by virtue of its human origins susceptible to error. Even so, this witness testifies to God who is against any ideology, norm, structure or value that serves the interest of the powerful by marginalising or dehumanising an individual or community.[15]

Given this understanding of God and God's purposes in our world, an approach that is critical and inclusive constitutes a "hermeneutical principle," an interpretative framework through which meaning is derived from biblical texts and according to which texts can be evaluated. Such a hermeneutical principle is consistent with theological understandings that the Bible's authority has Jesus Christ, the incarnate word, as its foundation. Correspondingly, the emphasis in considerations of biblical authority should be placed on "Jesus the Word made flesh which dwelt amongst us" and not just on the Bible as a written document.

> The Bible shares the incarnational character of the One to whom it bears witness, it proclaims by its composition as well as its declarations that the Creator has chosen to be revealed in creation, even coming among us as one of us. But that manifestation does not exhaust or circumscribe the divine presence or power, and the word by which that action is recalled and re-presented is only the servant of the living word. The words of God spoken to prophets and poets are essential to Christian faith and carry the authority of their Speaker, but the Word of God cannot be contained in any document; nor can it be comprehended apart from the Word made flesh, which is both the center and the norm of Scripture.[16]

People who endorse ideologies that seek to oppress for the benefit of the dominant do so by claiming divine sanction to their positions. They interpret the biblical text in such a way that it justifies their ideological

---

[15] Charles H. Cosgrove, *Appealing to Scripture in Moral Debate: Five Hermeneutical Rules*, Grand Rapids, MI: Eerdmans, 2002, 109.

[16] Phyllis Bird, "Authority of the Bible," 63.

positions. Conferring a divine origin to the biblical text not only serves their interests, but also reinforces its authority and deems it unquestionable. There is certainly something appealing about such a position, but on the flip side, it ensures that the human involvement in the production of the text is minimised or completely rejected. As a divine product, the Bible becomes static, infallible and beyond critique, demanding absolute obedience.

In today's pluralistic world, we can no longer accept a single and particular interpretation offered by a single community or individual. There is growing resistance to anyone or anything that claims to represent the whole. Through the voices and literature by marginalised people and communities, those who are different by virtue of caste, gender, class, sexual orientation and religion, God is indeed shaking the foundations. What is timeless, supreme and unchanging is God's commitment to justice. Whatever diminishes the full humanity of a person does not reflect the divine. With an inclusive hermeneutic, the word of God has a deeper meaning that goes far beyond the simplistic literal one.

## Conclusion

By heeding to the voices of the marginalised, we participate in and continue God's work of redemption and reconciliation. Empowered by the Holy Spirit, those of us who follow in the name of Jesus Christ must work for the liberation and transformation of structures and systems. In fact, the whole meaning of Scripture is embedded in this divine encounter for justice. I readily concede that this is only one way of reading scripture. But I am convinced that incorporating the realities and struggles of the marginalised majority is a theological and missiological imperative that we must pay attention to.

Chapter 5

# Role of Churches in Nation-Building

*Roger Gaikwad*

## Discussion in 1960: Fifty Years Ago

Between 1950 and 1960, during the crucial foundational years after Independence, churches in India discussed the issue of their participation in nation-building. These discussions were summed up in the book titled, *Christian Participation in Nation-Building*, which was jointly published in 1960 by National Christian Council of India and Christian Institute for the Study of Religion and Society. The preface to this book begins with the following words:

> With political independence India has entered a period of national development. She has given herself a democratic constitution and is building up the political structures of a Nation-State. She has set her face to increase agricultural productivity, industrialize the country and enhance the nation's standard of living, through a planned process of economic development. She is also seeking to direct and control the changes in the structures and values of the joint-family, caste, village and other traditional institutions of common life, with a view to developing new patterns of community. All

these changes in the political, economic and social realms constitute a veritable revolution and ask for new religious and cultural foundations.¹

It was in the context of such euphoria about the imminent socio-economic and political revolution that it was remarked:

> The Christians and Churches of India are as much involved in this revolution of national development as any other Indian. How are they to relate themselves to it? ... The Church is concerned with the purpose of God for the world as revealed in Jesus Christ. And she is called to participate in the life and development of the nation, in order to witness to Jesus Christ as Lord and Saviour of mankind.²

The Christian response to the challenges of the socio-economic and political revolution, which was articulated in theological-Christological and missiological terms, had three important practical implications:

1. To work out the elements of a Christian understanding of certain crucial issues in the political, economic and social development of modern India.

2. To enter into conversation with socially-conscious people of other faiths, both secularist and Hindu, in order to consider together the nature of an adequate social philosophy for the new India and to work out the basis of Christian co-operation with them in social action.

3. To help the Church to rethink the pattern of its mission and service and to reorient its policies and programmes accordingly, with relevance to its social witness in a developing nation. ³

## What Is Indian Nation?[4]

The concept of India as a nation is said to be the creation of the British:

---

[1] M. M. Thomas (Compiler), *Christian Participation in Nation-Building: The Summing Up of a Corporate Study on Rapid Social Change,* Social Concerns Series No.9, Bangalore: NCCI & CISRS, 1960, p iii.

[2] *Ibid*, pp. iii-iv.

[3] *Ibid*, pp. vi-vii.

[4] A simple definition of nation would be a "group of people who share culture, ethnicity, and language, often possessing or seeking its own independent

Much good is often mixed with much evil. The British brought the old sub-continent of India under their political authority and sowed the seeds of nationhood and rule of law. The Indian Civil Service Code and introduction of British legal ideas and practices played a large part in this. The modern universities produced a class of people with an all-India outlook, educated in the English language and well-versed in the liberal writings from Locke to Laski, and committed to democratic ideas. This new Indian intelligentsia could detach itself from the narrow sectional loyalties of region, caste and religious community. It led the nation in its struggle against the British Raj, awakened the people to a sense of nationhood and educated them in the values of political freedom and democratic government....

The peaceful manner in which independence was gained and government ultimately transferred into our hands ensured that there was no break in the continuity of democratic institutions in India. And the framers of the Indian Constitution wisely decided to build upon the foundations already laid. The administrative unity introduced by the British rule was consolidated to a remarkable degree after Independence, particularly through the integration of the princely States in the Indian Union.[5]

---

government." As such, a nation is not necessarily equated with 'country' in that a country is akin to a 'state', which is defined as the political entity within defined borders. Because they are shared, the national population also has a degree of uniformity and *homogeneity*. And finally, at least some of the characteristics must be *exclusive*—to distinguish the nation from neighbouring nations. <http://en.wikipedia.org/wiki/Nation> (accessed on 7.10.10)

Some ideas of nation do not emphasize shared characteristics; rather they emphasize shared or mutually agreed choice for membership. Therefore some say that a nation is first and foremost an idea. It is an idea that springs from the expression of a natural human desire for a community of people with common values and for freedom from dominance over the will and desires of its people in their pursuit of happiness. <http://www.realnation.com/what_is_a_realnation> (accessed on 7.10.10)

Although *"nation"* is also commonly used in informal discourse as a synonym for *state* or *country*, a nation is not identical to a state. Countries where the social concept of "nation" coincides with the political concept of state are called 'nation states.' <http://en.wikipedia.org/wiki/Nation> (accessed on 7.10.10)

[5] *Ibid.*, pp.1-2.

While the political movement to throw off the British yoke cultivated the concept of Indian nationhood and the British legacy of political administration, law, educational system, etc. facilitated the coming into existence of the state of India, the concept of India as a nation has been subject to challenges. Though the constitution of India prohibits it, the history of India has seen quite a good number of secessionist movements in Jammu and Kashmir, Nagaland, Mizoram, Punjab, Assam, Manipur, Tripura and Tamil Nadu.[6] In some states, these movements have died down because of a mixture of military action and political agreements. However, the problem still persists in the psyche of the people, the distinctiveness of their race and culture and their struggles for identity, dignity and community rights. Since their problems are not resolved justly they still wonder whether they are part of India and whether they could consider themselves or be considered Indian.

During the past thirty years or so, the country has also witnessed the rise of so many regional political parties and movements that one wonders whether 'India' really matters: people assert their ethnic identities or socio-cultural, politico-economic concerns over and above their Indian belongingness. Right wing political parties, cultural organisations and religious groups further heighten the problem with fundamentalist and communal activities. When electronic media instantly (indeed 'live') broadcast the horrifying pictures of communal and other kinds of violence, one wonders whether India is really a land of pluralistic harmony, a land of unity in diversity. However, when one focuses one's attention on the world of sports, entertainment or war, in which India is participating, one is surprisingly impressed by the show of Indian solidarity. Again, when one sits in the comfort of one's house and watches cultural programmes of different regions of India, one is quite proud of today's India.

So what is this Indian nation we are talking about? It should be remembered that India, as it stands today, is not one homogenous country. Historical, political, constitutional and economic factors have made us what we are today. In spite of all the diversities that cause problems

---

[6] <*http://en.wikipedia.org/wiki/Secession#India*> (accessed on 7.10.10)

(without in any way condoning the injustices perpetrated on certain regions, nor being insensitive to the sufferings inflicted on different communities), it is best that in the contemporary context, we continue to remain a united country. India is to remain a 'country of countries.' In one sense, it would be apt to call it the 'United States of India.'

## What Kind of Nation-Building Are We Talking About?

Jochen Hippler, a political scientist, observes that nation-building was a key concept of foreign, security and development policy in the 1950s and 1960s, in particular. At that time, it was closely linked with the modernisation theories that understood and explained the development process in the Third World in terms of catching up with Western models. Third World countries would have to be 'modernised'; their structures would have to be adapted to the industrialised countries by converting 'traditional' or 'tribal' societies into 'modern' nation-states. The European model implicitly or explicitly was the intended goal. 'Nationality' and the 'nation-state' were fundamental categories, with economic and political development regarded as promising success only in this context.[7]

'Nation-building' was also construed in the 1950s and 1960s, in the context of the East-West conflict, to be a western strategy for containing socialism and the Soviet Union in the Third World. In the same way, as other concepts, it was intended to represent an alternative to the victory of liberation movements and the 'revolution.'[8]

However, the term 'nation-building' sunk into oblivion during the 1970s. Compromised by the constant emphasis of it in the Vietnam War, its association with military strategies and its conceptual link with markedly brutal political forms of "pacifying" the country, it became unfashionable both politically and academically. To pursue the goal of winning the "hearts and minds" of the Vietnamese people, units of the United States Army, referred to as "Civil Affairs" units, were used extensively for the first time since World War II. Civil Affairs units, while

---

[7] http://www.jochen-hippler.de/Aufsatze/Nation-Building__Concepts/nation-building__concepts.html (accessed on 07.10.10)

[8] Ibid.

remaining armed and under direct military control, engaged in what came to be known as "nation-building": constructing (or reconstructing) schools, public buildings, roads and other infrastructure; conducting medical programmes for civilians who had no access to medical facilities; facilitating co-operation among local civilian leaders; conducting hygiene and other training for civilians; and similar activities. This policy of attempting to win the hearts and minds of the Vietnamese people, however, was often at odds with other aspects of the war, which served to antagonise many Vietnamese civilians. These policies included the emphasis on 'body count' as a way of measuring military success on the battlefield, the bombing of villages and the killing of civilians in such incidents as the My Lai massacre.[9]

Nation-building again came to the fore in the 1990s. In 1992, the USA along with the UN intervened to stop the brutal civil war and immense suffering in Somalia. In 1994, the United Nations approved military intervention in Haiti to restore the elected President, whom the army had overthrown. President Clinton sent in American troops, who joined with smaller forces from other countries. They established order, abolished the Haitian army, trained a national police force and oversaw elections. In the late 1990s, President Clinton authorised American military forces to work with the United Nations and North Atlantic Treaty Organization (NATO) to end ethnic conflict and genocide in the Balkans, particularly in Bosnia and Kosovo.[10] Today's USA is engaged in so-called nation-building exercises in Iraq and Afghanistan. Nation-building thus seems to be largely a military exercise.

And here we are talking about nation-building in today's India. Paraphrasing Jochen Hippler's words, one may say that the task of nation-building in India has three important requirements:[11]

---

[9] http://en.wikipedia.org/wiki/Opposition_to_the_U.S._involvement_in_the_Vietnam_War (accessed on 7.10.10)

[10] http://www.crf-usa.org/election-central/nation-building.html (accessed on 7.10.10)

[11] http://www.jochen-hippler.de/Aufsatze/Nation-Building__Concepts/nation-building__concepts.html (accessed on 07.10.10)

(1) Nation-building will only be successful in the long term if it stems from an *integrative ideology* or produces this from a certain point on. As long as people in a region define themselves primarily as Brahmins, Marathas, Tamils, Mizos, or members of a particular clan, nation-building has either not been concluded or has failed. The existence of the respective identities is not in itself the problem but their relationship with a "national" identity covering all groups. However, as long as the primary identity and loyalty lie with the caste, tribe, clan or an ethnic or ethno-religious group and the "national" identity level remains subordinate or is missing, a nation-state will continue to be precarious.

(2) The second prerequisite for a successful nation-building process involves the *integration of a society* from the loosely associated groups that existed previously. The Malayalees, the Gujaratis and the Punjabis must be convinced that they belong to a common nation, and this notion must also be found in the social reality.

(3) The third prerequisite is the development of a functional state apparatus that can actually control its national territory. *State-building* is a key aspect of successful nation-building. It presupposes a range of practical capabilities, such as creating a financial basis for a functioning state apparatus, i.e., an effective fiscal system, as well as an organised police and legal system and an administrative apparatus that is effective and accepted throughout the country. The state needs loyal personnel that do not identify primarily with individual, social, ethnic or religious communities but, rather, with the state and the "nation." In particular, the state apparatus must assert its monopoly of force over the entire national territory in order to be successful over the long term.

## Importance of Nation-Building in the Context of Globalisation

Nation-building becomes a concern of vital importance in the contemporary context of globalisation. Rapid advances in technology (especially the computer and digitisation), communication (such as fibre optic cables, satellites and the Internet) and transportation have made the whole world a small village. With these advances, geography, as a social barrier, has been transcended and many aspects of social life (conversation, buying, selling, art, literature, music, philosophy, religion, politics, economics, etc.) are carried out on a global scale. These different facets of globalisation are challenging the identity and sovereignty of nations.

Particularly, economic globalisation [the matrix of international and multinational corporations, international money markets, global agribusiness, intra-global trade, free trade zones, international trade agreements (WTO, NAFTA, etc.), international economic organisations (IMF, World bank, G7), economic unions (such as European Economic Union), the interaction of economically diverse partners and the extremely volatile global capital markets] has altered the traditional political landscape. Nations must now contend with multinational corporations, whose operating budgets are much larger than those of many nations (eg. General Motors has a larger economy than that of Denmark or Thailand; Ford Motors is an economic rival to Hong Kong, Turkey, Saudi Arabia, etc; the economies of Poland or Israel cannot match up to those of Exxon or Wal-Mart; then again the economies of IBM, General Electric and Mobil are far superior to those of Columbia, Iran, and many Third World countries).

As a result, the identity of nations is changed. They are no more nations; they are considered as 'markets.' Presently, India is considered to be a very lucrative market. The people of India are not citizens; they have been reduced to being 'consumers.' The traditional understanding of national sovereignty has been threatened. Nations are now accountable to and have to negotiate with corporations and organisations that are based outside their own countries and which are quite often economically more powerful than them.

Related to the phenomenon of economic globalisation is the expression of cultural globalisation. The whole world having become a global village, we are being drawn to relish eating American burgers, Italian pizzas and Chinese noodles. At the same time, Indian food dishes are being presented in new flavours—mainly to draw international attention. Similar is the case when it comes to clothes and dressing, architectural design and interior decoration. Then again we have the phenomenon of people crossing boundaries and dwelling together, thereby giving rise to more and more ethnically mixed societies. Such a situation raises the question: Should we still be obsessed with asserting cultural nationalities or should we not opt for and advocate one-world cultural integrity? Is not nation-building an old-fashioned outdated concept? In spite of all the instances and trends of trans-border cultural expressions, it is rather strange that the world is experiencing the self-assertion of identities by numerically small ethnic, religious and other communities. It is the political perspective that dominates, though culturally, socially and technologically there is a lot of inter-mingling.

## Role of Churches in Nation-Building: Fifty Years Ago and Now

### Christian Participation in Political Life

Fifty years ago, the corporate study made the following observations: "Some groups of Christians have regarded this idea of political participation with disfavour, on wrong scriptural and doctrinal grounds. They interpret the Gospel in purely spiritual, otherworldly, or individualistic terms and forget that it is the message of Christ's salvation to the whole of life, including politics, that is, our organized life together."[12] The situation is no different now. The content of the songs sung and messages preached during 'Praise and Worship' sessions in general foster the otherworldly emphasis and the spirit of individual benefit and prosperity. Such a perspective continues to subscribe to the dualistic view of the earthly political realm belonging to Satan, while the other world belongs to Jesus the King; so they have nothing much to do with participation in political life except praying (as per the biblical direction) for those in political authority and for peace when there is violence in and among nations and perhaps exercising franchise during political elections (giving to Caesar the things that are Caesar's!).

The Corporate Study, however, sought to correct such perspectives and practices: "The Gospel of Christ cannot in intention be non-political. It is the proclamation of the Kingship of Jesus Christ over all areas of the life of mankind, a Kingship that today is seen and declared by faith, but will be openly manifested at the end of times. Therefore, Christian participation is not an obligation laid on us by the nation; it is also part

---

[12] M. M. Thomas (Compiler), Christian Participation in Nation-Building, p.48.

of our obligation to our Lord Himself. He has ordained our earthly citizenship so that in exercising its responsibilities, we may express our loyalty to his Law and witness to His love."[13]

This Christological perspective on political responsibility, very significant as it seems to Christians, could in contemporary pluralistic contexts sound as communal to Hindu ears as the concept of Ram Rajya would sound to Christian ears. Therefore, it is important to emphasise the concept of the reign of God, characterised by love, justice, responsible relationships and wholistic growth. Jesus himself preached about the reign of God (and not his reign). His entire life was theocentric: "I have come to do the will of him who sent me" (John 5:30). The focus should be on moving towards an all-embracing community of God/Truth seekers and followers: "Many will come from east and west and sit at table with Abraham, Isaac, and Jacob in the kingdom of heaven" (Matt. 8:11), a vision of a God-centred ecumenical community given to us by Jesus himself. The qualification for entry into such a kingdom, which Jesus himself spells out in Matt. 25:34-36, is not the practice of a particular religion, or the following of a particular doctrine, but the discerning of God's solidarity-presence among and liberating concern for the suffering and needy in this world. Again Jesus says that when one works to bring healing and reconciliation in the world, then indeed the finger of God is at work, and God's reign finds expression in our midst (Luke 11:20).

The Corporate Study made noteworthy methodological suggestions for Christian participation in political life: "In a country where communalism is the bane of politics the Christian community should not organize itself as a Christian political party to fight exclusively for its own communal interests. Nor should the Church or a congregation, as such, identify itself with any one of the political parties. This, however, does not preclude the Church or the Christian community lending active support to a specific programme of one political party wherever such a programme is understood to be serving the larger interests of the country. There is also a case for the Church warning people against totalitarian

---

[13] *Ibid.*

parties, which are organized explicitly on principles incompatible with the Christian principle of reverence for the individual person."[14]

"On the other side, there is need for organized effort in educating the Christian community in political matters, and helping its members to enter more actively into the secular democratic parties of the country. Without this organized effort, Christians will not become politically alive."[15]

Such propositions have several practical implications: forming political study circles or citizenship groups, conducting seminars on political education, expressing opinions on all matters of national importance and making them known to the political authorities, supporting and cultivating the constitutional concept of a secular state, working for the fulfillment of nationalist goal of establishing a socialist pattern of society, informing members of State assemblies and parliament of Christian views on national/state issues, advocacy of noble and just causes, publishing literature on political questions, etc. These programmes could be implemented not only at the local church level, but also at state, regional and national levels. National ecumenical organisations like NCCI, YMCA, YWCA, SCMI and CISRS and their regional bodies and local units could also play an effective role in this regard. A suggestion was also made to set up a civic organisation of Christians on an all-India basis.[16]

Beyond forming Christian civic organisations the emphasis should now be on Christians being part of and participating in civil society movements. The term 'civil society' denotes the totality of voluntary civic and social organisations and institutions (such as registered charities, development non-governmental organisations, community groups, women's organisations, faith-based organisations, professional associations, trade unions, self-help groups, social movements, business associations, coalitions and advocacy groups) that form the basis of a

---

[14] *Ibid.*, pp.49-50.

[15] *Ibid.*, p.50.

[16] *Ibid.*, pp.52-58.

functioning society, as distinct from the force-backed structures of a state and commercial institutions of the market.[17]

## Socio-Economic Challenges and Christian Responsibility

Fifty years ago, the Church made a very laudable contribution to the nation through educational institutions, medical services, technological training centres, orphanages, old people's homes, facilities for the blind, houses for juvenile delinquents, etc. In today's India, there are several such services that are provided by the government and several non-governmental organisations. If the Church is to continue with such ministries, it has to ensure high standards of service without commercialising those ministries. At the same time, the Church is called to advocate for alternative economies, technologies and ways of life. In other words, in a groaning world, the Church has to take the lead in offering hope of life, of eco-human health, of just-peace, of inclusiveness for all those who are living on the margins of society and of wholistic growth. The Church has to permeate society with values of the reign of God.

However the Church cannot do all this by itself. The need of the hour is for the Church to join hands with like-minded and like-committed bodies. As has often been said, religions divide, but service unites!

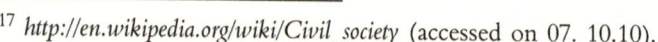

---

[17] *http://en.wikipedia.org/wiki/Civil_society* (accessed on 07. 10.10).

Chapter 6

# Promotion of Social and Economic Equality in India by the Church as Participation in Mission of God

## Sunil Michael Caleb

As disciples of Jesus Christ, it is fundamental to our belief that God has a will and purpose for the world that God seeks to establish in co-operation with human beings who have been created in God's Image. A shorthand way that Jesus used to define this will and purpose was to speak of the bringing near or the coming of the 'Kingdom of God.'[1] There will obviously be different ways of reaching the goal of God's reign in every area of our lives. What those different ways should be, each people group, nation, church and local congregation has to discover.

It is the duty of every generation to prayerfully search for the mind of God as to what is to be the Mission of God in their particular situation.

---

[1] In our contemporary situation, where kings are rare and where democracy is more common, we have nowadays begun to speak of the 'reign of God' instead of the 'kingdom of God.' This is apart from the fact that the term 'kingdom' is speaking exclusively about the rule of a male King, when quite evidently God has no particular gender.

Almost a hundred years ago, there was the World Missionary Conference in Edinburgh that attempted to speak to its generation. One hundred years on, it is imperative that we attempt to look to our situation and ask how we can bring closer the reign of God. Participation in the implementation of the reign of God will be participation in the *Missio Dei* for our time. Since the reign of God as shown by Jesus is taking care of those who are pushed to the margins of society by the powerful, the participation in the *Missio Dei* must be a process of looking at the provision of abundant life from the perspective of those living on the margins of society.

One of the very significant features of our time is the presence and growth in inequality both in the social arena and the area of economic matters. It is the argument of this paper that such inequality goes against the establishment of the will of God because it harms the strengthening of community, which is the original will and purpose of God. Since the establishment of community is the goal and purpose of God, inequality in the social sphere and in the economic sphere must be fought against because these inequalities complicate the formation of community.

In the first section of this paper, I shall establish the extent of inequality—social and economic—that exists in India. In the next section I will attempt to show how inequality is against the will of God, because it complicates the building of community. In the third and final section, I will try to answer the question as to how we are to participate in the mission of God, which is to struggle against the forces that perpetuate inequality.

## Economic and Social Inequality in India

India is one of the most 'unequal' countries of the world. Only a small minority in India has the standard of living that the upper classes of developed countries have. The majority of people in our country do not have enough to eat; they lead shelterless lives, with no access to education and medical care. South Asia is the only region in the world where the caste system exists—and the caste system breeds nothing but inequality.

## Material Inequality in India

In India, social inequalities are largely reflected in material inequalities. The vast majority of the poor in India consists of landless labourers, small and marginal farmers and rural artisans. The vast majority of these people have been identified as Scheduled Castes (Dalits) and Scheduled Tribes.[2] So when we look at the material situation of the Dalits and the Tribals, we get an accurate picture about the extent of poverty and inequality in India.

## Economic Inequality

In India, there is tremendous disparity between the rich and the poor. India is home to some of the richest persons in the world as well as to the largest number of malnourished children in the world. In 2009, India had 126, 700 dollar millionaires.[3] At the very same time, of the estimated 120 million children under five in the developing world that are underweight (that is deficient in weight for age—a composite measure of stunting and wasting), close to 54 million are children in India.[4] Further, the proportion of underweight children is the highest among the Scheduled Tribes at 55 per cent, 48 per cent among the Dalits and 43 per cent among the OBCs and 34 per cent among others.[5] And it seems that this situation is not improving, even though we are told that India is one of the fastest growing economies in the world and that India is only second behind China in annual GNP growth. The noted economist, Utsa Patnaik, writes:

> The National Sample Survey data on consumption show that between 1993-94 and 2004-05, over 60 per cent of India's rural population has seen a substantial absolute decline in the intake of both cereals and animal

---

[2] James David, 'Globalisation: Impact on Dalits and Tribals' in Chandran Paul Martin (ed.) *Christianity, Wealth and Poverty: Indian Perspectives,* Nagpur/Delhi: NCCI/ISPCK, 2004, p.21.

[3] *http://www.dnaindia.com/india/report_india-has-126700-dollar-millionaires_1400486 accessed on 29/09/2010.*

[4] Cited in A.K. Shiva Kumar, 'Stunted India' in *Frontline,* Vol. 27(2010) No.8, p. 4.

[5] *Ibid.,* p. 5.

products, such as milk, eggs and meat, while the top 10 percent registered a sharp rise in animal product intake though not in cereal intake.... The percentage of persons unable to obtain a daily energy intake of even 2,200 calories rose from 58.5 per cent in 1993-94 to 69.5 per cent in 2004-05 and the position is probably worse now.[6]

On the other hand, we see an increasing trend towards obesity in wealthy urban children in India. Though no all-India figures are available, anecdotal evidence and micro-level studies show that obesity among children of the well-to-do is rising fast. One study done over a period of two years in Kerala found that the proportion of overweight children increased from 4.94 per cent of the total students in 2003 to 6.57 per cent in 2005. The increase was significant in both boys and girls. The proportion of overweight children was significantly higher in urban regions and at private schools, and the rising trend was limited to private schools.[7] Because this rapid increase was in urban areas and only among children attending private schools, we can be sure that this rise in obesity is occurring among the rich minority of Indians. A very sure indication of this rising trend of obesity among the urban rich is seen in the huge jump in various kinds of slimming centres where people try to reduce their weight. Newspapers are full of advertisements for gyms and products that help people reduce their weight.

In the early 1980s, at the all-India level, about 58 per cent of the Dalits were poor as compared with 37 per cent of non-Dalits/STs. Between 1983 and 2000, the incidence of poverty declined in all the social groups at the all-India level and in all the states, but at a lower per annum rate for the Dalits (2 per cent) as compared to non-Dalits/STs (3.3 per cent). Thus, the decline in the level of poverty was associated with a corresponding rise in the inequality between the two groups.[8] As V. K.

---

[6] Utsa Patnaik, 'A world of distress', *Frontline*, Vol. 24 (2009) No.7, p.13. (Emphasis mine).

[7] Manu Raj, K. R. Sundaram, Mary Paul, A. S. Deepa, R. Krishna Kumar, 'Obesity in Indian children: Time trends and relationship with hypertension' *National Medical Journal of India Vol 20(2007) No. 6*, pp.288-293.

[8] Sukhdeo Thorat. *Dalits in India: Search for a Common Destiny*, New Delhi: Sage, 2009, p.95.

Borooah points out, "At least one-third of the average income probability between Hindu (dominant castes) and SC/ST households was due to 'unequal treatment of the latter.'"⁹

As Pranab Bardhan, Professor of Economics, University of California, Berkeley, has pointed out, according to estimates by the Asian Development Bank (2007), the Gini coefficient of average real wages of urban full-time employees in India increased from 0.38 in 1983 to 0.47 in 2004. This increase in wage inequality is mainly due to the fact that high economic growth in India has been very skill intensive and been in a sector like Information Technology (IT), which needs a high level of education and training.¹⁰ However, this shows that there has been considerable growth in inequality of wages among the people living and working in urban areas in India

*Land Distribution*

As mentioned above, the Dalits and the Tribals constitute the vast majority of the poor in India. So, data on land distribution among the Dalits gives us a good proxy for estimating the distribution of the land among the poorer classes. The majority of the Dalits living in rural areas work as agricultural labourers. In 1999-2000, about one-third of the Dalit rural labour households owned land, as against 41 per cent for all rural labour households. The landowning rural labour households were largely concentrated in the land size category of less than 0.40 ha. Their concentration in the farm size categories of 0.4-1.0 ha and more than 1

---

⁹ Cited in Vani Kant Borooah, *Caste, Inequality and Poverty in India*, Review of Development Economics, Vol 9 (2005) Issue 3, pp. 399-414. Taken from the Internet-based abstract of the article. Accessed on 05.10.10.

¹⁰ Pranab Bardhan, *Awakening Giants: Feet of Clay*, p.98, http://books.google.co.in/books?id=WvgW3B3XEsAC&printsec=frontcover&dq=pranab+bardhan+on+economic+inequality&source=bl&ots=YT1OlAHU43&sig=jYdTCQkCHfB1m5kxCFQJFODFc&hl=en&ei=5kurTNv_DsaXcd3IjdsE&sa=X&oi=book_result&ct=result&resnum=3&ved=0CCUQ6AEwAg#v=onepage&q&f=false, accessed on 05 October 2010. In the Gini coefficient, the numbers are between Zero and One, Zero denoting perfect equality and One denoting complete inequality. Thus the higher the coefficient, the higher the inequality.

ha was particularly low for the Dalits (6.6 per cent and 2.3 per cent, respectively) compared to all-rural labour households (9.4 per cent and 3.5 percent, respectively). Due to the small size of the landholdings, the Dalits had to turn to wage employment in a much greater magnitude than non-Dalit groups.[11] Thus, the pattern of landownership is skewed against the Dalits. Since the Dalits have very limited access to land, it could be that they are able to make up by a higher proportion engaging in employment. However, statistics show that even this is not so. As Pranab Bardhan has pointed out, when land quality is taken into account in its valuation as is done by the National Sample Survey Assets and Liabilities Survey data, the Gini coefficient of ownership of asset distribution was 0.63 in 2002 in rural India, while the corresponding figure for China was 0.39 in the same year.[12] This is an extremely high level of inequality.

## Employment and Unemployment

According to the Current Daily Status statistics of the National Sample Survey reports in 1999-2000, the all-India employment levels of the Dalits and non-Dalits/STs in rural areas indicate that the employment rate of Dalit males in rural India was 46.2 per cent, whereas the figure stood at 48 per cent for non-Dalit/ST males. However, employment for rural Dalit females was higher at 21.1 per cent as against 18 per cent for non-Dalit/ST females.[13]

Though the Dalits account for 16.2 per cent of the Indian population (2001 Census), and 15 per cent of central government jobs were reserved for them, in 2003, the percentage of the Dalits was only 11.9 per cent in Group A jobs and 14.3 per cent in Group B jobs.[14]

---

[11] Sukhdeo Thorat. *Dalits in India: Search for a Common Destiny,* New Delhi: Sage, 2009, p.63

[12] Pranab Bardhan, 'How unequal a country is India' http://business.rediff.com/column/2009/sep/07/how-unequal-a-country-is-india.htm accessed on 05 October 2010.

[13] *Ibid.,* p.63.

[14] *Ibid.,* p.74.

## Inequality in Education

The literacy status of the Dalits in India is terrible. The census of 2001 indicated that they constitute about 20 per cent of the 300 million illiterate Indians—far in excess of their share in the population. In 2001 only a little more than 5 per cent of the Dalits aged 20-24 had education beyond higher secondary. Their presence in vocational courses was miniscule. On the other hand, more than 10 per cent of non-Dalit/ST men and women attended colleges, which was almost double the percentage for the Dalits.[15] According to World Bank estimates, the Gini coefficient of the distribution of adult schooling years in the population, a crude measure of educational inequality, was 0.56 in India in 1998/2000, which is not just higher than 0.37 in China in 2000, but even higher than almost all Latin American countries (in Brazil, it was 0.39)—mainly because of India's large illiterate population.[16]

## Inequality Based on Caste

Even when people of different castes in India are economically of the same level, we find that they are treated unequally solely because of their caste status. We have read of cases where even Dalit IAS officers were not treated properly by their peons who were of a 'higher' caste. In certain districts, Dalit children attending school are made to sit separately from other children, taught in a perfunctory manner and not allowed to drink from the common school water tap. Even within the church in India, there is inequality, with there being cases of separate cemeteries for the Dalits and separate seating arrangements in church and separate distribution at the time of the Eucharist.

Not only is material inequality bad for those that are at the bottom of society but social scientists have shown that such inequality has a deleterious effect upon many social and psychological indicators such as crime and rates of depression. A very significant new study in this regard is the work of Richard Wilkinson and Kate Pickett entitled, *The Spirit Level: Why more equal societies almost always do better.* In this book, Wilkinson

---

[15] *Ibid.*, p.104.

[16] Pranab Bardhan, *How unequal a country is India. Op. cit.*

and Pickett study the effects of inequality in and across 23 wealthy countries and the 50 States of the United States of America (USA). Using data from various studies they show how income inequality leads to a poorer quality of life for all people in these countries and states of the USA and they put forward the significant contention that "greater equality is the material foundation on which better social relations are built."[17] Thus they show how greater income inequality leads to lower levels of trust, which damage community relations.[18] They examine countries that have higher levels of income inequality and find that these countries also have a higher level of mental illness and use of illegal drugs.[19] Even health in the rich countries that they study is significantly affected by income inequality with "Inequality [is] associated with lower life expectancy, higher rates of infant mortality, shorter height, poor self-reported health, low birth weight, AIDS and depression."[20] Their main contention in this regard is that income inequality leads to chronic stress among those who have a low status leading to various health problems and lower levels of life expectancy. They also discover that countries with greater Income inequality also have higher levels of violence at all levels.[21]

Having established that there is considerable inequality in India and then seen how even social scientists are saying that material inequality is detrimental to societies, we now turn to look at what could be the perspective of God on this situation, thereby coming to some conclusion as to what could be the mission of God in the current situation in India.

### God's Mission for Community and Greater Equality

A careful study of the biblical view would prove to us that two words, 'community' and 'equality' are fundamental to the purpose of God as revealed in the Bible. A study of the work of God among the peoples

---

[17] Richard Wilkinson and Kate Pickett, *The Spirit Level: Why more equal societies almost always do better*, London: Allen Lane, 2009, p.265.

[18] *Ibid.*, pp.60-62.

[19] *Ibid.*, pp. 67-70.

[20] *Ibid.*, p.81.

[21] *Ibid.*, pp. 129-144

described in both the Hebrew Bible and the New Testament will show that it is the goal of God that God's created beings live together in a community of justice, fairness and love. It is as if the aim of God is to create a community of love that is like the community of love that constitutes the Holy Trinity; the sharing that is present within the Godhead is to be replicated in our life on earth in communities of love and sharing.[22] How can this be substantiated?

In the creation story in Genesis, we read that the first man and the first woman were made in the image of God. Since each human being is created in the image of God, it is obvious that human beings are of equal value; they may not have the same intelligence, strength and so on, but they have the same value in the sight of God. Right from the creation of humankind there was no place for inequality, be it on the basis of gender, race or economic status. Thus the basis upon which God wanted to create community was the equality of value of each and every human being.

God has, of course, not left Godself without witness in every age and in every land, but as followers of the Lord Jesus Christ we are the inheritors of a faith-tradition that began in what are now the lands of Palestine, Israel and Egypt. So we look especially for the actions of God in the scriptures that came out of these lands.

The people who came to be known as the Jews were fundamentally formed by an event in which they were liberated from bondage in Egypt. And the goal of liberation was to form a community in the mould of God's will and purpose. As Paul D. Hanson states, "God's deliverance of a slave people inaugurated a new order of life for Israel and, concretely, a new notion of community. Israel began to draw out some of the cardinal qualities of that new order as the Israelites lived in the wake of this memorable foundational event."[23] As Walter Brueggemann writes:

---

[22] Cf. Geevarghese Mar Osthathios, *Sharing God and a sharing world,* Delhi: ISPCK, 1995.

[23] Paul D. Hanson, 'The Birth of the Covenant' in Max Stackhouse, Dennis P. McCann and Shirley J. Roels (eds.), *On Moral Business: Classical and Contemporary Resources for Ethics in Economic Life,* Grand Rapids, Mich: Wm. B. Eerdmanns, 1995, p. 59.

> Israel is a 'social experiment' in the world of the Ancient Near East to see if a community can be organized in egalitarian (covenantal) patterns, in resistance to the hierarchical, bureaucratic modes of the world of the city-states. The alternative model of social organization seeks to distribute power so that all members are treated with dignity, so that all members have access to social goods and social power.[24]

It was then to maintain this community that in the pre-monarchy phase of Israel various kinds of laws and commands were put into place that limited the kind of inequality that was allowed to develop. And it was precisely because of the fact that economic inequality and social inequality led to the undermining of the idea of community upon which the people of Israel had been founded, that such laws and commands were proclaimed. Since individuals would act as if wealth and power belonged to them and not to God, there were always the possibilities of large inequalities opening up. The result would be a divided community or society where there were rich and poor, the landed and the landless, free and slave, debt holders and debtors.[25] In other words, a class (and even caste) society would develop. In order to counter these tendencies, prophets and leaders were inspired to set in place laws and customs that would rectify the mistakes that were inevitable. As Timothy Gorringe informs us:

> The proposed answer to this problem was the Jubilee legislation. Every seven years (Deuteronomy) or ever fifty years (Leviticus) debts must be remitted, and families returned to their patrimony. In this way, class society would be periodically deconstructed.[26]

The teaching and practice of Jesus too had this emphasis upon community and equality. He chose twelve apostles from different backgrounds as the founding nucleus of the new communities that he was proposing; communities of love under God. All his teaching was summed up in the

---

[24] Walter Brueggemann, *A Social Reading of the Old Testament: Prophetic Approaches to Israel's Communal Life,* ed. By Patrick D. Miller, Minneapolis: Fortress Press, 1994, p.58.

[25] Bob Holman, *Towards Equality: A Christian Manifesto,* London: SPCK, 1997, p.7

[26] Quoted in *Ibid,* p. 7.

two greatest commandments, namely "Love your Lord your God with all your heart, with all your soul, and with all your mind. And Love your neighbour as yourself" (Matt. 22:37-39). If there was ever a divine pointer to the desirability of equality, it is this. We are to grant to our neighbours the advantages that we give ourselves. And further from the Parable of the Good Samaritan (Luke 10:25f.) we see that our neighbour is the one who needs our help and can even be a person whom we would not usually associate with or even treat as an enemy. So, community and the equality that will encourage this community is a vision that is central to the teaching and practice of Jesus.

The early church too practiced community and sought to maintain equality in order to strengthen the feeling of community. Thus as we read in Acts of the Apostles, believers who had more than others sold what they had in order to meet the needs of those of the early Christian community that were in need (Acts 2:44, 45).

The concern for community and equality is something that is also found in the writings of St. Paul. In his second letter to the Corinthians, chapter eight, Paul writes about the collection of relief for the famine-hit Christians of Palestine. While urging the churches of Corinth to be generous, Paul says that it is necessary, in order that there be equality (*isotes*). He then goes on to refer to the passage in Exodus where the Israelites were in the wilderness and were supplied manna by God. At that time the amount of 'manna' that each Israelite household was able to collect was equal, since "those who gathered much had nothing over, and those who gathered little had not shortage; they gathered as much as each of them needed." Thus Paul suggests that there be community feeling between the believers in Corinth and those in Palestine and that could happen only when there was sharing and greater equality between these two groups of people. Inequality is not the appropriate base for the formation of community.

A further example of Paul's emphasis upon community and equality is found in his discussion of the Eucharist found in his first letter to the Corinthians chapter eleven. Here Paul condemns the conducting of a Eucharistic meal where there is a social division between the rich Christians who arrive early and eat, not waiting for the poorer believers, who because of the nature of their work, arrive later. As he writes, "When you come together, it is not really to eat the Lord's Supper" (I Cor. 11.20). As Demetrius C. Passakos states, "We could paraphrase Paul in his *(sic)* facing of the problems in the Eucharistic gathering: 'Do you want your gathering to be a truly Eucharistic one? Then you should have equality and justice in the community!'"[27]

From these selected examples, I think it is clear that the Mission of God has to do with the establishment of community. This maintenance of community requires that inequalities be reduced to a minimum because differences in wealth and in social status are destroyers of community. It is obviously not necessary that the removal of economic inequalities or inequalities of social status will automatically lead to the establishment of the kind of community life that God has intended for humankind. However, while it is not a sufficient condition, I believe that I am right in saying that it is a necessary condition.

## Participation in the Mission of God

Given that search for social and economic equality is participation in the mission of God, it is now our task to find ways in which we can work with God to reduce inequalities. India faces economic, educational and social inequalities. Removing these inequalities is therefore participation in the mission of God.

### *Mission against Economic Inequality*

Inequalities in economic matters usually arise from differences in the distribution of the assets that people use in order to earn a regular stream of income. These assets are land, financial assets and even educational qualifications leading to a skill. Thus, a big landlord will obviously earn a larger stream of income than is the case with a landless labourer. The inequality in the income arises from the fact that one has land while the other does not. So, in this case, participation in the *Missio Dei* would mean participation in the struggle for the redistribution of land, inspired by the kind of legislation found in Leviticus 25. Here we see that every

---

[27] Demetrius C. Passakos, 'Eucharist in First Corinthians: A Sociological Study', *Revue Biblique* 104 (1997), p.205.

fifty years, the land that has been lost by a person, for whatever reason, is returned to him and those who have taken that land, for whatever reason, must return it. Similarly, from Deuteronomy 15 we learn that every seventh year debts were to be forgiven. These laws were placed in the Torah in order that the tendency towards inequality in wealth among the people of Israel would be nipped in the bud and not go out of control. Learning from these biblical laws, participation in the mission of God would involve pressing governments to redistribute land between those who already have plenty of land and those who have none. It would involve pressing for schemes that involve the forgiving of unpayable debt, especially by those who are poor. It would involve asking governments to redistribute income through higher taxation on high-income earners and wealthy people and subsidies to those who have lower incomes and lower wealth.

## *Mission Against Caste Discrimination*

Participation in the mission of God in order to bring greater equality in the social field in India will definitely involve a struggle against the caste system. The struggle will involve stressing the equality of all human beings and challenging religious justifications of the caste system, if any. All areas where discrimination is practiced will have to be challenged so that equality is achieved in the social sphere and the community that God has planned for each one of us is realised. In case there is discrimination on the basis of caste within the church, it must never go unchallenged. Participation in the mission of God will involve agitating against the practice of giving occupations such as manual scavenging and cleaning of service latrines to the Dalits, so that such occupations are banned.

In India, social and economic inequalities have been preventing the formation of the community that God has planned for each one of us. So, participation in the *Missio Dei* would involve challenging this inequality.

Chapter 7

# Indigenous Dalit and Tribal Missiologies and Missiologists

## Siga Arles

I am grateful to ISPCK for giving me the opportunity to participate in this Mission Consultation in the context of its jubilee celebrations. It is a joy to meet with fellow Christians concerned with the Mission of the Church and its priorities and challenges. I congratulate ISPCK for its years of publishing service and contribution to the life and witness of the Church in India and wish a brighter future of greater service in enhancing the witness by providing relevant literature to educate the church.

I will present this paper by, firstly, identifying Missiology as a subject; secondly, locating the study of Missiology within Indian theological education; thirdly, enlisting the scholars that emerged as missiologists from among tribal Christians and Dalit Christians; and, fourthly, discussing the indigenous quality of the kind of Missiology developed by these missiologists. Finally, we will consider the way forward in developing indigenous Missiology from Dalit and Tribal scholars.[1]

---

[1] This paper was presented at ISPCK Tercentenary Mission Consultation in Delhi.

## Some Clarifications

The indigenous people of India are the 'original' people of India. We must note that there is a strong claim made by the Dravidians, particularly the Tamils, that the Dravidians were the original inhabitants of India; they lived in Indus Valley and developed the Harappa Mohenjodaro Civilisation; the Aryans from Central Asia came and pushed the Dravidians to move down South to the Deccan Plateau, where now the Dravidians predominate the modern four States of South India—the Tamil, Telugu, Kannada and Malayali people groups.

The original people are known as the *adivasis*. They were the native folk. They were animists who worshipped the powers of nature such as *prithvi, jal, agni, vayu* and *akash* (earth, water, fire, wind and space). Later, Aryans who settled at Indus Valley and developed Hinduism made an imposition of their Hinduism upon the Dravidians. Such Hinduism brought along with it the tendency and tenacity to divide people on the basis of caste, paving the way for a certain proportion of people to be identified as, earlier, the *mlechchas,* untouchables, *harijans* of Gandhiji and later the modern Dalits with lesser social status.

It is commonly stated that the Dalits responded more positively to the Christian gospel and entered the Church in search of freedom and equity. Educational uplift enabled this community to rise in social status. Through the nineteenth and twentieth centuries impact of the gospel on them in terms of education, they became the leaders of the church in India by default. It is also commonly stated that since the dalits suffered generations of oppression and servitude, they were not ready for leadership. When they assumed roles of leadership, they were ill equipped to measure up. While there may be room for this criticism, there are ample examples of Dalit Christians rising up to match the demand of leadership. The transforming power of the gospel has enabled many of them to rise up like eagles and to march in step with others who presumed superiority by birth.

The term *adivasi* is also applied to the primal people or the tribal folk in the hills, jungles and plains. It was customary to hold them as 'primitive' and backward. Yet education and mission activity has brought about tremendous transformation among them. For instance, the Nagas,

Mizos, Khasis and such have made rapid progress in education and lifestyle and are spread all across the nation and the globe into comfortable settings.

Both the dalits and the tribals are *adivasis*—indigenous people with their age-old customs and culture. The affect of the gospel accompanied with western education and colonial impact did not necessarily imply a deculturisation process. To be Christian did not have to mean to be non-Indian or anti-Indian. Though forces within the tribal community aroused at times anti-national ethos, the ongoing journey of the Christian tribals has consistently been patriotic and indigenous.

Christian dalits and tribals have a missionary calling to nation-building and need regular motivational input and training in order to get involved meaningfully. The Church's ministry should primarily be to equip the laity for their mission in society.

## Identifying Missiology as an Academic Subject

"Is Missiology an academic discipline?" asked the Dutch Professor Jan Jongeneel[2] while tracing the origin and development of the subject.

> Missiology is the discipline which deals with 'mission' as its subject-matter. The term 'mission' – [a non-biblical term] as a technical term – was coined by the Jesuits. Ignatius of Loyola (1491-1556), the founder of the *Societas Jesu*, stated that all members of the Society must be willing to be sent to their special fields, i.e., to their 'divisions' or 'missions'... 'destinations'... 'territories'....
>
> The term 'missiology' is rather new. It was coined by the Dutch Jesuit Ludwig J. van Rijckevorsel in 1915.[3]

Jongeneel traces how Roman Catholics used the term but Protestants criticised, opposed and later accepted; and how the subject area grew in theological institutions and university departments. Jongeneel states:

---

[2] Jan Jongeneel, "Is Missiology an Academic Discipline?", *Exchange*, A journal of Missiological and Ecumenical Research, 27:3, Reprinted in *Transformation*, July 1998, pp27-32.

[3] *Ibid.*, p27.

> Missiology is the academic discipline which – from a philosophical, empirical, and theological point of view – reflects upon the history, theory and practice of (Christian) world mission as a means for both preaching the gospel, healing the sick and casting out 'evil spirits' (active in idolatry and immorality), for the glory of God and the well-being of all human beings.[4]

Lutheran North American Church Historian James A. Scherer considers the definitions of many noted scholars to identify "Missiology as a Discipline and [goes on to discuss] What It Includes."[5] According to him, it is an inclusive subject that roots in biblical studies and church history, relates to systematic and contextual theologies, religions, philosophies and social sciences and integrates with all of knowledge and truth. It also is exclusive in that it is a subject in itself that stands on its feet independently. Scherer says: "Missiology must find a way to be holistic, integrative, inclusive, and complementary to human learning without becoming *exhaustive*."[6]

Justine Anderson argues for the rightful place of Missiology within Theology:

> Theology is a living organism rather than a hodgepodge of separate studies. Its subdivisions, such as apologetics or missiology, cannot, and should not, be radically separate. Nevertheless, there remains every reason to accept the science of missions as an independent entity. It has become an essential element in the theological curriculum.... Missiology must continue to develop its theological relationship with the other disciplines in order to maintain its hard-earned place in theological education.[7]

Further, James Scherer stresses that:

> Missiology has an *integrating and permeating* role to play within the theological curriculum. Mission is seen as central to the whole life of the church. Everything done in the seminary should be permeated by the sense of mission. In this sense, mission can be taken as the real organizing principle

---

[4] *Ibid.*, p28.

[5] See *Missiology: An International Review*, XV:4, October 1987, pp507-522.

[6] *Ibid.*, p514.

[7] Justine Anderson, "An Overview of Missiology" in John Mark Terry & et.al. (eds.), *Missiology: An Introduction to the Foundations, History and Strategies of World Missions*, Nashville: Broadman and Holman Publishers, 1998, p4.

for the theological curriculum. Missiology ought to play the role of catalyst in seminaries and challenge theological education to be faithful to its true calling. For "mission is the mother of theology".[8]

## Locating the Study of Missiology in Indian Theological Education

Firstly, let us take a quick survey of "Theological Education in India"[9] and then identify the study of mission and Missiology within it.

### Early Beginnings of Theological Education in India

Tradition says that even within the first century St. Thomas established seven churches in South West India in the modern Kerala area, for which the ministry was trained in informal style as junior men became apprentice disciples to be trained by the senior pastors.[10] After a long period of inactivity and no missional growth of the church in India, the Roman Catholics arrived in sixteenth century counter reformation mood with Francis Xavier at Goa and systematically established their mission and ministry training programme through their many Orders and have grown the largest Christian faction in India.[11] The first Protestants were the German Lutherans at Tranquebar Mission in 1706 who initiated Tamil New Testament translation and the first catechist and clergy training.[12]

---

[8] [As stated by Martin Kaehler]. James Scherer, "The Future of Missiology as an Academic Discipline in Seminary Education: An Attempt at Reinterpretation and Clarification", Report of a Survey of ATS-related schools in USA on the Current Status of Teaching of Missions, in *Missiology*, XIII:4, October 1985, p457.

[9] See Siga Arles, "Theological Education in India", *Contemporary Christian*, 2:1, August 2010, pp20-29.

[10] The best and cheapest available book to read to know of early developments is Cyril B Firth, *An Introduction to Indian Church History*, Madras: CLS (Text Book Series of Serampore, no.23), 1961, reprint 1983, pp304.

[11] See "The Roman Catholic Mission, 1600-1787" Chapter 6 in Stephen Neill, *A History of Christian Missions*, London: Penguin History of the Church, Volume 6, 1964, reprint 1990, pp151-178.

[12] See Arno Lehmann, *It Began at Tranquebar*, Brijraj Singh, *The First Protestant Missionary to India: Barthalomaeus Ziegenbalg, 1693-1719*, Delhi: Oxford University Press, 1999, pp195. Cf. George Oommen and Hans Raun Iversen (eds.), *It Began in Copenhagen: Junctions in 300 years of Indian-Danish Relations in Christian Mission*, Delhi: ISPCK, 2005, pp436.

The British Baptists arrived led by William Carey in 1793 and opened the first college for all of Asia—Serampore College in 1818, which later grew to be the mother institution for theological education of the mainstream Protestant churches of India and neighbouring countries.[13] Anglicans built the Bishops College in Calcutta (Kolkata) in 1820. The Reformed, the Methodist, the Presbyterian and the Congregational as well as the Baptists set up their own training institutions through the nineteenth century. During this time, ministerial training was "elementary", "denominational", "male" and characterised by its "isolation from the general trend of academic education" in the country.[14]

## Developments during the First Half of the Twentieth Century

Two major developments in the beginning of the twentieth century were significant in the journey of Theological Education in India. Firstly, the renewal of the Serampore Council and the initiating of the Affiliation process by the Senate of Serampore College which gave a national structure to develop, guide and govern TE.[15] Second was the establishing of the United Theological College at Bangalore in 1910 by the co-operation of several mission societies to develop a training programme with better facilities of library and faculty to cater for leadership development.[16]

---

[13] See George Howells (ed.), *The Story of Serampore and Its College*, Serampore: College Council, 1927, pp116. Cf. Wilma Stewart (ed.), *The Story of Serampore and Its College*, Serampore: College Council, 1960, pp124.

[14] See A. D. Lindsay, *Report on Christian Higher Education in India*, London: OUP, 1931, p237.

[15] For an account of this, see George Howells, *Op.Cit.*, Ch.VI and Wilma Stewart, *Op.Cit.*, Ch.IV.

[16] Since UTC is celebrating its centenary, there are publications planned that will help provide you with the history, development and contributions of UTC to Indian theological education. See J. H. Maclean, "The History of the College" in *The Bangalore UTC Magazine*, Silver Jubilee issue, 4:1, October 1935. Cf. Russell Chandran, "The First Fifty Years of the College" in *Fifty Years of Service 1910-1960*, Golden Jubilee Volume, 1960.

International Missionary Council (IMC) motivated National Christian Council of India to interpret the identity, mission and effectiveness of the Christian Colleges including five of the BD level Theological Colleges in 1928. The report[17] indicates the great growth of educational and missionary/ministerial training. Within a decade after that, IMC again inspired NCC to make a survey of theological and biblical training institutions in India. Charles W. Ranson led the study from Tambaram 1938, and the report *The Christian Minister in India* of 1945 proves the first major source of information on the status of theological training in India.[18] Here again the denominational, regional, elementary and male clergy orientation was heavy. Only a decade later, in 1955, M H Harrison Report[19] refers to the first entry of women into theological training through a specialised institution such as Christhu Seva Vidyalay, Chennai. It also informs of the initiatives to set up colleges in local languages to promote relevant training for ministry. Through the next decades emerged Tamil Nadu Theological Seminary (1969), Kerala United Theological Seminary, Andhra Christian Theological College and Karnataka Theological College—all in South India where Christian presence was considerably higher.

### *Developments during the Second Half of the Twentieth Century*

There were two kinds of institutions. Firstly, the colleges of the mainstream churches that were affiliated with the Senate of Serampore College. Secondly, the Bible Schools of the many denominations that were of lower standard and were keenly identified as evangelical in their perceptions and did not seek affiliation with Serampore. They did not wish to be shaped and controlled by Serampore. National Council of Churches of India initiated its Board of Theological Education (BTE) to bring these institutions into a co-ordination and offered accreditation under BTE.

---

[17] A. D. Lindsay, *Report of the Christian Higher Education in India, Op.Cit.,*

[18] Charles W. Ranson, *The Christian Minister in India,* London: Lutterworth Press, 1946, pp317.

[19] See M. H. Harrison, *After Ten Years – A Report on Theological Education in India,* Nagpur: BTE-NCCI, 1957, pp71.

When the Missionary Movement under IMC gave birth to the Ecumenical Movement in the World Council of Churches in 1948, the evangelicals viewed the increased emphasis of unity that they feared was minimising the emphasis on evangelism and mission, and so, they set up World Evangelical Fellowship (WEF) in 1951 to safeguard evangelism and mission. This paved the way for a global polarisation within the church. Sadly, there developed competitive and duplicating emphases of the ecumenicals and evangelicals. The church has to be innately evangelical and innovatively ecumenical if it should be true to the gospel! The Church of South India is rooted in evangelical faith and operates with ecumenical width. This ought to be the rightful emphasis in the way we shape the church. The sixties saw the worldward journey of ecumenical Missiology that took the social realities seriously and interpreted mission and theology from contextual concern. Theological Education Fund (TEF)[20] motivated the pursuit after contextual theology and thus, contextual theological education. These were significant positive developments that impacted the developments of theological education in India. To cite an example, the Principals Samuel Amirtham and Gnana Robinson of Tamil Nadu Theological Seminary (TTS) were at the major TEF consultations in Manila and took the impetus for contextualisation and shaped the theological education at TTS with creative boldness.

Evangelicals soon formed Asia Theological Association (ATA) in 1970 more from a defensive mindset.[21] Paralleling TEF, WEF initiated Theological Assistance Programme (TAP) and helped to provide incentives to shape evangelical theological education—as though in separation and isolation. Many Indian institutions that identify themselves as evangelical withdrew from Serampore affiliation and became accredited

---

[20] See Christine Lienemann-Perrin, *Training for a Relevant Ministry: A Study of the Work of the Theological Education Fund,* Madras: CLS for PTE/WCC, 1981.

[21] See ATA History in the writings of Bong Rin Ro in *ATA News,* published by him during his time of service for ATA from Taiwan. ATA while celebrating its fortieth year at the General Assembly in Hong Kong, in August 2010, released its history edited by Bong Rin Ro, Ken Gnanakan, Joseph Shao, Bruce Nicholls, et.al., *New Era, New Vision: Celebrating 40 Years of the Asia Theological Association,* 2010.

by Asia Theological Association. The next forty years saw an uneasy and unhappy development of ecumenical TE under Serampore and evangelical TE under ATA. This certainly was a duplication of efforts and proved divisive. What makes it a pain is the fact that there are quite a few colleges that are affiliated with Serampore, which are 'evangelical' by choice. Serampore, though often assumed as 'ecumenical', is inclusive of ecumenical and evangelical emphases. At present, we have about 45 colleges affiliated with Serampore and a dozen institutions linked with Board of Theological Education; and about 60 colleges accredited by ATA with 30+ colleges as associate members. In all of these, we may have about 100,000 students undergoing theological training for the ministry of the church.

Though quite a number of Pentecostal colleges are found in SSC and ATA, there are many more that either have come under a NATA (National Association for Theological Accreditation) or a NAPTE (National Association for Pentecostal Theological Education) or IATA (International Association for Theological Accreditation) or are in direct link with one of the North American Theological Colleges. Korean missions have come into India in a big way and are also setting up their own institutions either in link with one of the above streams or independently.

From the fifties, there had been a mushrooming of indigenous missions of India, which by now are more than 500 (at least half of them are members of India Missions Association). Many of them have developed their missionary training programmes, centres and institutions. Several of them come under Indian Institute of Missiology (IIM), which in keeping with a global trend has registered itself as Indian Institute of Inter Cultural Studies. IIM has developed itself into an imitation of Serampore system and offers degrees in Mission studies. Several of the parachurch ministries have their own training programmes that are variously linked with the existing structures of TE, either fully or partially or not at all.

What we refer in the above two paragraphs adds up to a considerable number of institutions for theological and missiological education in India. Evening Bible College and Theological Education by Extension have also become a growing phenomenon. There could be several hundred Bible Schools—upwards of 600—Missionary Training Institutions and short-term, non-degree Evangelism training programmes spread across India. These perhaps are catering for another 100,000 men and women.

Thus, theological education happens in India in several streams: (1) Serampore, (2) ATA, (3) Pentecostal, (4) Missionary Societies, (5) Parachurch Ministries and (6) linked with foreign colleges or universities.

Most of the training that prevails in Indian Christian community seems to be catering for the training of grassroots-level workers. Bible colleges and seminaries train the next higher levels of evangelists, pastors and teachers. Dr. David Bennett of Boston, USA, was commissioned by Funding Agencies of USA to study the leadership training needs in India during the transitional years of 1998 to 2002. He saw five levels of leaders of whom he found the lower three levels being catered for. But the top two levels had very little avenues of training. The CEOs, the Professors, the top officers were lacking training programmes for them. It was in that context in 2002 that we set up a Consortium for Indian Missiological Education (CIME) as a Ph.D. Centre in Missiological Research Studies. I directed it and was the Dean for five years till 2007 and we graduated five candidates with Ph.D. degrees.[22] This was to help develop faculty of Missiology for evangelical colleges. Then I helped to set up Indian Institute of Missiology Research Centre (IIMRC) to develop leaders with

---

[22] The theses written by the five graduates are: (1) Ebenezer Dasan, *The Impact of the Gospel on the Adivasis of South Gujarat: An Investigation into the Mission Methods*, Bangalore: Centre for Contemporary Christianity, Studies in Gospel interface with Indian Contexts No.11, 2009, pp373. (2) Hetoni Swu, "The Mission of the Sumi Baptist Church in the Emerging Socio-Economic Context of Nagaland", 2006; (3) Samuel Saravanan, "Saurashtrians of Tamil Nadu: Patterns of Rejection and Acceptance of the Gospel of Jesus Christ", 2006; (4) Pari Titus, "Female Infanticide in Madurai, Salem and Dharmapuri Districts of Tamil Nadu and its Implication for Christian Mission", 2007; ( 5) Joshua Jaechul Lee, "An Analysis of Korean Missionary Training in Relation to the Requirements of Missionary Service in the Pluralistic Settings of South Asia", 2008. CFCC expects to publish all these theses in its Context Series.

MTh and PhD study options for the Missionary Training programmes of India Mission Association. Currently, I direct Centre for Contemporary Christianity, which has an academic wing continuing to offer PhD as well as MTh in Missiology for working people as an extension study. We also started another subject area—Holistic Child Development. And soon we wish to offer the prospect of extension study in other needy fields, where we lack leadership and professors: Church History, Counseling, Religions and Contextual Theology.

## *An Assessment*

Though Serampore has had its MTh and ThD programmes, it has not produced enough people in all the branches. There is severe poverty for teachers in departments such as Religion, Counseling, New Testament, Homiletics, Christian Education, etc. ATA has not developed post-graduate studies except in Missiology at about five centres, Theology at three centres, Church History at two centres and Pastoralia, Biblical Studies and Religion at just one centre each. Most of them are not strong as they lack residential teachers. Faculty development is an urgent need. In the other streams, there are plenty of either honorary or cheap degrees that are obtained without real education. This lowers the standard and so is an unwelcome development in theological education in India.

Today, the population of India is over 1.1 billion (1,100,000,000). The Christian population is normally said to be 3 per cent = 33 million. But including the followers of Christ outside the church (churchless Christians/unbaptized/secret believers), the number is proposed to be 6 per cent by some = 66 million; and few take it all the way to 10 per cent = 100 million. It is hard to be accurate about the number. At times, it is better to ignore the number, as it frightens the majority community of the Hindus and it works against Christian interest to draw attention of the Hindutva outfit.

Whatever the number, the training of a ministry to the existing church is the task of theological colleges and the training of a missional outreach to those outside the church is the challenge to the mission training structures. As mentioned above, both the processes are happening in India in multiple ways.

Even if we need ONE Christian worker for every ONE THOUSAND people, then for the 1.1 billion Indians, we will need 11 million Christian workers! What we have is far short of this number. The existing 33 or 66 million Christians will then have to work to develop one out of three or one out of six Christians as full time Christian workers. This will be impossible. Tent makers will have to each take a proportionate number to reach with the gospel. The training of such tent makers will be the challenge for the future of the mission of the church in India.

### Some Observations on Theological Education in India

- Polarisation of theological trends due to the dividedness of the church in India is a weakness that affects the formation of relevant theology to motivate the total church for a holistic mission in India. Need for convergence and ecumenicity is being acknowledged and there are attempts to pull together.

- During the Seventies, the need for contextualization of Theology was emphasised by TEF. During the eighties the BTESSC and SATHRI Doctoral Programme enabled research students to explore into contextual theology in their theses. By the Nineties, there were several theses written on Dalit Theology, Tribal Theology and Feminist Theology as contextual theological explorations. The search for a relevant theology as the mood of the age is revealed in the doctoral thesis of Franklyn J. Balasundaram: *EATWOT in Asia: Towards a Relevant Theology*.[23] The thesis of M. T. Cherian is an example of how the doctoral theses are attempting to look at contextual issues. He took up *Hindutva Agenda and Minority Rights: A Christian Response*.[24] It should be fair to assess that Indian theological education is addressing life issues and attempts to make sense of the gospel to Indian situation. In this process, there is much hope for the future of the Gospel in India.

---

[23] Subtitle of the thesis: The Ecumenical Association of Third World Theologians and the Development of the Christian Thought in Asia: A Historical and Theological Interpretation, Bangalore: Asian Trading Corporation, 1993, pp342.

[24] SATHRI thesis of 2003. Published by Bangalore: Centre for Contemporary Christianity, 2007 & 2010.

- More post-graduate centres are needed to develop all departmental faculty and leadership for the future. What is available is inadequate for the growing church.

- The church in India is still struggling to meet its own theological leadership need and has not sufficiently felt the need for its global mission. Whereas there is a decline of faith and the numerical strength of the church in the northern hemisphere, and whereas the centre of gravity of the church has moved to the southern hemisphere, particularly in Africa, Latin America and Asia, there is need for Asia/India to take its role in supplying missionaries to the wider world and to the Indian Diaspora around the world. See the plight of Indian Christians in North America and their attempt to discover their mission in their new homeland as interpreted in *Pilgrims at the Crossroads: Asian Indian Christians at the North American Frontier,*[25] a report from two consultations held at Princeton Theological Seminary.

- Theological search for understanding the mission of the church in India is actively carried out in many quarters. This is revealed in the kind of mission publications from the many centres of learning, research and publications in India.[26]

## Study of Mission and Missiology in Theological Education in India

In the theological colleges affiliated with Senate of Serampore, the BTh and BD student has basically one course in which 'Mission, Witness and Evangelism' are defined and introduced. But three courses in mission at BD level are required of a BD graduate who wishes to specialise in Missiology in MTh study. The course in Indian Church History and History of Ecumenical Movement, which are compulsory courses in BD, are counted as the two other courses to fulfil the requirement. But this is unsatisfactory. The fact remains, there is insufficient mission study

---

[25] See Anand Veeraraj & Rachel McDermott (eds.), *Pilgrims...,* Bangalore: CFCC, 2009, pp. 256.

[26] For a summary presentation, see Siga Arles, "The State of Mission Studies in India: An Overview and Assessment of Publications and Publishing" in *International Bulletin of Missionary Research,* 34:3, July 2010, pp. 156-164.

within the theological curriculum, which exists in the colleges of Serampore.

ATA colleges tend to give courses in Church Growth, Cultural Anthropology and other subjects relating to mission. Yet they are taught with a mission history and missionary training slant rather than mission theology and contextual/contemporary rethinking. More of mission courses are offered at Missionary Training Institutes including linguistics, translation, cross cultural communication and missionary biographies. Only at MTh level 'Missiology' is explored into. As already mentioned, doctoral-level Missiology is rare and recent. So, Missiology as an academic discipline is not strong in India. As a result, the developing of missiologists had been rare.

Every theologian specialises in an area and often looks down at the subject area of mission. But while visiting the West, each turns into a missiologist! Since they speak to the West about the church and mission in India, they gain some interest in mission and Missiology; they even enquire to learn the subject.

As noted above, Missiology has some sort of an existence only at the post-graduate level of study. MTh in Missiology was started in 1982 at ATA (SAIACS) and in 1992 in Serampore (Union Biblical Seminary). Prior to this, few individuals went to study in places such as Fuller, Asbury, Trinity, Dallas and such theological seminaries in USA and studied either a Masters or Doctor degree in Missiology. Some went to Missions Academy in Germany but returned to teach Old Testament or other subjects. Specialisation in Missiology was unknown in India till the last decades of the twentieth century.

## Missiologists from among Tribal Christians

Every theologian is a missiologist—that was the sort of understanding that prevailed in India. Thus, among Tribal Christians there were several who were identifiable as contextual theologians and so, missiologists. A leading voice among them was Renthy Keitzer, Principal, Eastern Theological College, Jorhat, Assam, who took the concept of contextualisation of theology and proposed the process of *Naganisation* of the Christian gospel. Similar was the call of Alem Ao, Principal, Clarke

Theological College, Mokokchung, to *Tsungremology*. His successor Takatemjen poetically captures the cry of tribal theology and mission:

> No more guns and no more wars,
> Only peace everywhere.
> No more tears and no more fears—
> That's my dream for the whole wide world.
> No more chains and no more sorrows,
> Only love everywhere.
> Singing songs of people set free—
> That's my dream for the whole wide world.[27]

Appealing to the contextual realities in Nagaland, the Tribal Studies programme undertaken from ETC with Wati Longchar and a host of others explored into the mission of the church and its challenges and published a series of books in quick succession:[28] *An Exploration of Tribal Theology, Traditional Tribal Worldview and Ecology, Doing Theology with Tribal Resources, Transforming Theology for Empowering Women, Encounter between Gospel and Culture, No More Guns! People's Struggle for Justice* and *An Emerging Asian Theology: Tribal Theology: Issues, Method and Perspective*. Further, Wati also offered *The Tribal Religious Traditions in North East India: An Introduction*, which along with the edited works of Saral Chatterji, *Society and Culture in North-East India: A Christian Perspective*,[29] Jesudas M Athyal, *Mission Today: Subaltern Perspectives*[30] and O. L. Snaitang, *Churches of Indigenous Origins in Northeast India*,[31] provide us with much information about the

---

[27] Quoted by Wati Longchar in the acknowledgement to his *No More Guns! People's Struggle for Justice,* Tribal Study Series No.7, Department of Tribal Studies, ETC, Jorhat, 2000.

[28] In the last decade of the twentieth century and the first decade of the twenty-first century, the Department of Tribal Studies at the Eastern Theological College in Jorhat published many books in a series as well as developed its Journal of Tribal Studies.

[29] Bangalore: CISRS / Delhi: ISPCK, 1996.

[30] Tiruvalla: Christava Sahitya Samiti, 2001.

[31] Chennai: Mylapore Institute of Indigenous Studies / Delhi: ISPCK, 2000.

place and process of tribal theology and its mission. In the many volumes cited above, various authors have addressed the issues and attempted to identify the theological insights and missiological methods in the process of ministry, such as V. K. Nuh, K. Thanzauva, R. L. Hnuni, V. Xaxa, N. Limatula Longkumer, Takatemjen, Roger Gaikwad, Ezamo Murry, Yangkahao Vashum, Peter Haokip and others.

Those who studied Missiology directly should be identified. C. L. Hminga studied the impact of the Gospel on Mizo people for his doctorate in Missiology at Fuller. Though his work was published[32] and he was associated with MDiv programme with William Carey Bicentenary efforts, he was not identified as a missiologist. The Mizo scholar to get that identity was Fanai Hrangkhuma, who after his MTh taught Church History at UBS and later obtained his PhD in Missiology from Fuller School of World Mission.[33] With him UBS started MTh in Missiology and he became the first architect to develop the curriculum and syllabii for MTh in Missiology for the Senate of Serampore. Later, he moved to Serampore and helped to start MTh in Missiology.[34] Another Mizo scholar who followed to teach Missiology was Lalsangkima Pachuau[35] who served for a short period at United Theological College and migrated to USA, where he teaches at Asbury Theological Seminary. These are the only two who could be counted as tribal Missiologists since their works are published and they have written certain number of articles and contributed to the shaping of Missiology. Others studied and taught but have not left a legacy through their writings.

---

[32] See C. L. Hminga, *The Life and Witness of the Churches in Mizoram*, Serkawn: Literature Committee, Baptist Church of Mizoram, 1987.

[33] "Mizoram Transformational Change: A Study of the Processes and Nature of Mizo Cultural Change and Factors that Contributed to the Change", PhD Dissertation, Fuller Theological Seminary, 1989.

[34] Both at UBS and at Serampore, Siga Arles succeeded Hrangkhuma and continued the MTh Missiology programme and thus stands the second person to develop the study of Missiology in Senate family.

[35] See his doctoral thesis *Ethnic Identity and Christianity: A Socio-Historical and Missiological Study of Christianity in Northeast India with Special Reference to Mizoram*, Frankfurt: Peter Lang, 2002.

Many have done their Doctor of Missiology and taught in seminaries such as Akumla Longkumer (Fuller / Clark) and Leaderwell Pohsngap (Asbury / UBS). Through the years of my own post-graduate missiological teaching, my students who studied mission in the context of tribal people include Rabi Pame, Krickwin Marak, Imti Wati, Marina Ngurzangzeli, Arjun Basumatary, Gilbert Borgoary, Temsu S, Toshirenba, Hetoni Swu, Vanlal Rova, Moatemsu, Watimongla, Jonali Doli, Vichuko Neikha, Meyigangla, Jonathan Chang, FC Beicho, Toholi Chishi and many more. From these Hetoni Swu completed her doctorate in Missiology through the Consortium for Indian Missiological Education; Arjun, Meyila, Beicho and Toholi Chishi are presently working on their doctoral research studies with the Centre for Contemporary Christianity.

For tribal Missiology, there are many who are developing theory and methodology and there is much hope as consistently many are being produced as missiologists. While this is true for North East tribes, for the plains tribes, Nirmal Minz[36] tops the list of those who addressed the issues and process of mission and theology. T. S. C. Hans, Agapit Tirkey and Telesphore P. Toppo have written on tribal concerns in the Jharkhand context.[37]

## Missiologists from among Dalit Christians

Who are the Dalits? There are at least three types of dalits:

1) The *original dalits* are those Scheduled Caste community of people who were considered as the untouchables, *harijans* and 'broken' people. They are the lowest of the social ladder of Hindu society. Among them there are many sub-divisions that assume a hierarchy and some consider the others as lower than them and ill treat, oppress or reject them. So, they would not inter-marry.

---

[36] See Nirmal Minz, *Rise Up, My People, and Claim the Promise: The Gospel among the Tribes of India,* Delhi: ISPCK, 1997. The poverty of the quality of the work developed is indicated even in the title of this book and the placement of the unnecessary commas. The author, editor and publisher have failed here.

[37] See their chapters in Jesudas M Athyal (ed.), *Mission Today: Subaltern Perspectives,* Tiruvalla: CSS, 2001, pp. 17-63.

2) The *occasional dalits* are those who at times will disassociate from the dalits but at other times identify themselves as dalits. For instance, the nadar community in South Tamil Nadu, who consider themselves superior to the paraya, ezhava and pulaya folk and would not intermarry. But in the global setting, such as in the World Council of Churches, they would allow themselves to be categorised among the dalits for whose liberation there are programmes and funds.

3) The *assumed dalits* are those who belong to the so-called upper-caste communities but show themselves as in solidarity with the dalits. The Syrian and Orthodox Christians of Kerala—particularly some in theological colleges—take such a stance and speak of dalit theology and at times teach dalit theology.

Let us also identify those who wrote, shaped and contributed to dalit theology. When Kunchala Rajaratnam opened the Department of Dalit Theology at Gurukul Lutheran Theological College and Research Centre in Chennai, Arvind Nirmal joined him and was considered the pioneer prophet of dalit theology. They promoted the cause of the dalits at a time when Senate of Serampore—in response to National Study of Theological Education in the 1970s—determined to increase the number of dalit and tribal candidates in post-graduate theological degree programmes. The National Seminars and the Summer Institutes of Gurukul took up dalit studies and the papers from them were published as a series of books edited by Arvind Nirmal and V. Devasahayam, such as *A Reader in Dalit Theology: Towards a Common Dalit Theology*, *Frontiers of Dalit Theology*, *Dalits and Women: Quest for Humanity* and *From "No People" to "God's People"*—all in the final two decades of the twentieth century. *Dalit Women's Experiences: A Theological Imperative for Indian Feminist Theology* was a posthumous publication of the thoughts of Prasanna Kumari Samuel of Gurukul in 2009. Gurukul took lead to shape dalit theology, which in turn did have implications for dalit Missiology.

Franklynn Jeyakumar Balasundaram of United Theological College engaged himself in verbalising the experiences of a few dalits. This was posthumously identified by his wife Elizabeth in a compilation of essays on those who attempted dalit theology, such as M. Azariah, M. E.

Prabhakar, Manohar Chandra Prasad, Maria Arul Raja, Monica J Melanchthon, Ruth Manorama and others.[38]

James Massey teamed with several to further the cause of Dalit theology through books such as *Indigenous People: Dalits – Dalit Issues in Today's Theological Debate*[39] and *Frontiers in Dalit Hermeneutics.*[40] His efforts are now developing Dalit Bible Commentaries with dalit interpretations.[41] Indukuri John Mohan Razu has written a few commentaries in this series.[42] ISPCK added many authors and their contributions to dalit efforts, such as John C. B. Webster, *The Dalit Christians: A History* (1992), Abraham Ayrookuzhiel, *The Dalit Desiyata: The Kerala Experience in Development and Class Struggle* (1990), Laxmi N. Berwa, *Asian Dalit Solidarity* (2000), J. A. David Onesimu, *Dr. Ambedkar's Critique Towards Christian Dalit Liberation* (2008), to name a few. In the series, we should also take note of non-ISPCK books. *Broken God Broken People: The Plight of Dalit Christians* by Manohar Chandra Prasad[43], *Dalit Pentecostalism: Spirituality of the Empowered Poor* by V. V. Thomas[44], *Dalit Empowerment* by Felix Wilfred[45], *M.M. Thomas and Dalit Theology* by Adrian Bird[46] and *Dalit Consciousness and Christian Conversion* by Samuel Jeyakumar.[47]

---

[38] See Elizabeth S. Balasundaram (ed.), *Dalits Speaking Experience,* Delhi: ISPCK, 2005.

[39] Edited work by James Massey in the ISPCK Contemporary Theological Education series, no.5. 1994.

[40] Edited with Samson Prabhakar, Bangalore: BTESSC / SATHRI & Delhi: CDSS, 2005.

[41] See the voluminous Dalit Commentary for the New Testament by Massey, Delhi: CDSS, 2010.

[42] See his commentary on *1 & 2 Maccabees, [Old Testament Volume 7]* Delhi: CDSS, 2012.

[43] Bangalore: Rachana Publications, 1996.

[44] Bangalore: Asian Trading Corporation, 2008.

[45] Bangalore: NBCLC, 2007.

[46] Bangalore: BTESSC / SATHRI, 2008.

[47] Oxford: Regnum, Delhi: ISPCK, 1999; Chennai: MEB, 1999.

*Endless Filth—The Saga of the Bhangis* by Mari Marcel Thekaekara[48] pierces through one's heart and jolts one's mind as the plight of the human persons involved in clearing human filth is reflected upon:

> 'In the rainy season,' began Leelaben, 'it is really bad. Water mixes with the shit and when we carry it on our heads, it drips from the baskets on to our clothes, our bodies, our faces. When I return home, I find it difficult to eat food sometimes. The smell never gets out of my clothes, my hair. But then in summer there is often no water to wash your hands before eating. It is difficult to say which is worse.'

Yesudas Moses appeals for the liberation of such people through the demand for change of laws governing working conditions of people caught by their dalitness into professions that inflict indignity.[49] Similar contextual theologians should emerge to tackle the many missional challenges that the church faces in the Indian situation.

There had been a partnership of the dalits and non-dalits in shaping dalit theology. Theology naturally leads to Missiology. Many of the authors cited above will not claim to be missiologists per se. But they are surely missional in their thought and involvement. Most of those who are missionaries per se also do not claim to be missiologists but mission activists.

Thus, from among the Dalits, it is hard to identify technical missiologists. Qualified academicians with Ph.D. are rare—I am perhaps at the top of the list as I have been teaching from 1975 and taught as visiting professor at most of the post-graduate centres where Missiology is offered in India. Through the number of M.Th., D.Miss. and Ph.D. students whom I mentored, which number crosses a hundred by now, and through the number of books and articles edited and published through my Centre for Contemporary Christianity, I have become known as a missiologist but not as dalit missiologist! Certainly, I am a dalit and a missiologist, but not a dalit missiologist. The only other person from dalit background who has taught in the field of Missiology at MTh level

---

[48] Bangalore: Books for Change, Action Aid, 2003.

[49] See reports of his *Safaikarmachari Andolan* and similar efforts.

in India is David Udayakumar of Gurukul. Many others from different fields of study have been involved in course teaching for Missiology students, but I cannot think of any who are identified as "missiologists." For instance, Abraham Christdas, Selvaraj, Chacko Thomas, Samuel Mathew, Jeyaraj Dasan, Ebenezer Dasan and a host of others (some of whom belong to upper-caste groups within the church).

## Indigenous Quality of Missiology Developed in India

Mission work in India has turned indigenous in funding, methods and motivation. This is so with structures such as the Friends Missionary Prayer Band and a host of others linked with India Missions Association. Most of them have resorted to devotional messages and literature to provide inspiration and incentive to mobilise supporters to mission activities. Missiology is not their concern as much as mission activity. Biblical foundations, History of Mission, Cross Cultural Mission, Cultural Anthropology, Bible Translation, Communication and Church Planting and Strategy for Church Growth are the areas of concern. Slowly and steadily, concern for the poor, economic development, justice, liberation and nation-building is emerging among mission societies. A few missionaries have gone on to study theology at the BTh level, and a few at the BD / M.Div. level. Some of them did MTh and those who explored doctoral study were no more involved in grass-roots mission. The distance has been created and maintained with suspicion.

The editorials I wrote for the journals I edited will suffice to indicate the type of Missiology that I propose to develop for India: "In Search of an Indian Missiology",[50] "Advocacy—A Missiological Iimperative"[51], "In Search of Relevance… In Search of Reality… In Search of the Real…",[52] "4/14 Window of the World: The Children@Risk",[53] "Another Missiological Challenge: Holistic Child Development",[54] "Glocal

---

[50] *Indian Journal of Missiology*, 7:1, August 2006, pp5-10.

[51] *Indian Journal of Missiology*, 8:1, August 2007, pp1-5.

[52] *Contemporary Christian*, 1:1, August 2009, pp5-9.

[53] *Contemporary Christian*, 1:2, November 2009, pp3-5.

[54] *Contemporary Christian*, 1:3, February 2010, pp3-6.

Theology in a Plural World Context",[55] "World Religion Database",[56] "A Call for Doing Theology in 21st Century Asia",[57] "Transform World: A Call of our Times",[58] "Theological Education: The 'Story' of Impacting Asian Pluralist Contexts",[59] "Theological Education in Asia: A Health Check",[60] "Each Congregation a Seminary: The Need for Team Ministry",[61] "Prophetic Voice of the Gospel in Contemporary Asia"[62] and "Mission Challenge—Bigger than ever in Asia!"[63]

As I work towards indigenous Missiology, I face a hurdle. It is the fact that the Church in India has been programmed by the impact of Western missions into its denominational divides and the major problem of polarisation as the Evangelicals and the Ecumenicals. The first problem was well tackled by the formation of the Church of South India in 1947[64] and the Church of North India in 1970;[65] but the second still remains active. Partly it is the funding from the Western and International bodies that perpetuate the division. Particularly in the Sixties and the Seventies, there was the development of parallel mission thoughts/missiologies. Ecumenical Missiology was world oriented with concern for justice, peace

---

[55] *Contemporary Christian*, 1:4, May 2010, pp4-7.

[56] *Contemporary Christian*, 2:1, August 2010, pp4-9.

[57] *Journal of Asian Evangelical Theology*, 11:1 & 2, June & December 2003, pp1-2.

[58] *Journal of Asian Evangelical Theology*, 13:1, June 2005, pp1-3.

[59] *Journal of Asian Evangelical Theology*, 14:1, June 2006, pp1-5.

[60] *Journal of Asian Evangelical Theology*, 14:2, December 2006, pp3-7.

[61] *Journal of Asian Evangelical Theology*, 15:1, June 2007, pp3-6.

[62] *Journal of Asian Evangelical Theology*, 15:2, December 2007, pp3-7.

[63] *Journal of Asian Evangelical Theology*, 16:1 & 2, June & December 2008, pp3-6.

[64] See Bengt Sundkler, The Church of South India: Movement Towards Union 1900-1947, London: Lutterworth Press, 1954.

[65] See Donald Kennedy, "The CNI History", *Indian Church History Review*, VI:2, 1972 and VII:1, 1973. Cf. Dhirendra Kumar Sahu, *The Church in North India: A Historical and Systematic Theological Inquiry into an Ecumenical Ecclesiology*, 1994.

and integrity of creation; and Evangelical Missiology was church-centric, church planting and church growth oriented. The two emphases need not be antithetical and operate as though from enemy camps. Thankfully the Eighties and the Nineties saw a willingness to relate and work together.[66] On the global level, Raymond Fung facilitated for the Commission on World Mission and Evangelism of the World Council of Churches to meet up with the representatives of the Evangelical movement at Stuttgart in 1987[67] and from then on there were several attempts of mutual learning and co-operation. The CWME at Athens in 2005 invited known evangelical and Pentecostal scholars to make plenary presentations, thus showing openness to the wider church. Though the Hindutva impact has pressured the church in India to go beyond divisions to present a united front to tackle the oppositions and attacks, there really does not exist a consistent warm relationship between the factions. Though NCCI, EFI and CBCI have co-operated in the capital to represent Christian concerns, the wider church remains divided at local settings with rarely any relationship or fellowship. Once in a while a Billy Graham Evangelistic Association programme or similar something may bring a meeting point, but the next may be several years away. The India Mission Association and its Indian Institute of Missiology have not at any occasion interacted with the Urban Industrial Mission of the National Council of Churches. The gap is widening here rather than narrowing. India Sunday School Union, All India Sunday School Association and Christian Education Department of Evangelical Fellowship of India remain aloof from one another and do not develop togetherness in their educational mission, except occasionally. Correctives are needed urgently.

So, rather than an active development of an indigenous Missiology suitable for India, we seem tied to our international links, which keep us apart—each protecting our views and concepts—essentially, safeguarding our budgets and resources. The majority part of the church

---

[66] See Donald Kennedy, *Light from any quarter? Ecumenical-Evangelical Studies in World Christian Mission*, Belfast: Ulster Services, 1982.

[67] Albrecht Hauser and Vinay Samuel (eds.) *Integral Evangelism*, Exeter: Paternoster / Regnum, 1988.

in India is claimed to be from the dalit stock and they are kept polarised and do not even realise this. We need to build a future of solidarity, unity, wider ecumenism and 'Ecumenical Relations.'[68]

## Way Forward

Postgraduate mission studies are less than thirty years old in India. Of those who obtained MTh, quite a large number are from the tribal and dalit backgrounds. Senate of Serampore-related MTh in Missiology rose and fell at UBS, NIIPGTS, UTC and GFABS. Gurukul struggles to maintain the department. More centres are emerging to offer postgraduate missiological degrees within ATA, such as SAIACS, ACTS Academy, HBI, COTRTS, Indian Institute of Missiology, Centre for Contemporary Christianity, etc. New initiatives, such as Academy for Church Planting Leadership, India Graduate School of Missiology and TAFTEE, also add to the list of centres of learning post-graduate Missiology. Qualified Indian faculty is an acute problem in sustaining these initiatives.

In my opinion, what is urgent is a systematic production of faculty members with doctoral qualification to teach Missiology. Serampore lacks a clear plan of action in this regard and other attempts are many and short-lived. Most attempts are what were initiated within the first decade of the twenty-first century, such as CIME, IIMRC, CFCC, AAHE, IGSM and TAFTEE. Fellowship of Indian missiologists had brought together missiologists into a fellowship for mutual inspiration. But it is predominantly of members from Roman Catholic background. Protestant missiologists—tribal and dalit, ecumenical and evangelical—must work together indigenously to pave the way for more and more specialists to emerge with doctoral degrees and set up centres of research studies and publications. The journey has started and there is much prospect for a healthy future for Missiology in the Indian subcontinent.

---

[68] See Siga Arles, "Ecumenical Relations" in Joseph Mattam and Joseph Valiamangalam (eds.), *Building Solidarity: Challenges to Christian Mission,* FOIM series no.XII, Delhi: ISPCK, 2008, pp223-231.

Chapter 8

# Urban Mission In India
## Transformational Engagement

*Richard Howell*

Cities critically determine the future of nations; their influence on the everyday affairs of individuals and communities is immeasurable. Nations, which comprise of business, education and government, have their power centres in cities. With an estimated population of 1.210 billion (2011), India's 27.8 per cent of urban population lives in more than 5,100 towns and over 380 urban agglomerations.[1] There has indeed been a massive increase in the urban population of India. Thirty-five cities have a million plus population, and 393 cities have a population of 100,000 and above. John Palen's comment is insightful: "The first years of the twenty-first century make a major transition to over half the world's population living in urban centres."[2]

---

[1] *http://en.wikipedia.org/wiki/List of states in India by past population,accesed*, 17 April, 2011.

[2] John Palen, *The Urban World,* New York: McGraw-Hill Book Company, 2002, 9.

The verdict of a billion citizens and tourists most aptly illustrates India, "as the most infuriating and the most hierarchical and the most degrading country in the world" while yet remaining the most interesting country.[3] Ramachandra Guha points to five transformations that are simultaneously taking place in India. "The Indian economy was once very largely based on agriculture; now, it increasingly depends upon industry and services. An overwhelming majority of Indians once lived in the villages; now hundreds of millions of Indians live in cities and towns. India was once a territory ruled over by Europeans; now, it is an independent nation-state. The political culture of India was once feudal and deferential; now, it is combative and participatory. The social system of India was once governed by community and patriarchy; now, it has had increasingly to make space for the assertion of individual rights as well as the rights of previously subordinated groups such as women and lower castes."[4] There is also a sixth transformation of religions that is underway. Old religious traditions are being challenged, and India is increasingly becoming religiously intolerant as visible from the persecution of its minorities.

## Process of Urbanisation

Though India is generally perceived to be a rural country, cities have been a part of it for centuries. Archaeological excavations show that India had a well-developed Sindhu civilisation with cities like Mohanjo Daro and Harappa. A number of ancient cities like Varanasi, Ranchi and Madurai have survived till today. Most of these ancient cities in India were either religious centres or political and administrative hubs of ancient India. During the British rule in India, the process of urbanisation picked up speed with the creation of 'cantonments,' which were well organised military, administrative and commercial centres of India. After limiting their activities to port cities like Mumbai, Kolkata and Chennai, 'district headquarters' cities were also developed. Urbanisation spread rapidly during the post-colonial phase with the emergence of industry in certain

---

[3] Ramachandra Guha, *Makers of Modern India,* Penguin Books India 2010, p. 4.

[4] Ramachanda Guha, *Makers of Modern India*, pp. 4-5.

regions of India. The most industrialised regions became the most urbanised regions.[5] "A discussion of urbanisation in India also involves rural-to-urban migration."[6] Social scientists call this the 'pull factor' in migration. Since urbanisation is an irreversible trend, we need to be adequately informed about emerging trends and be theologically equipped for undertaking ministry and mission among the growing urban population of India.

**Urban Church**

Looking at the contemporary Christian scene in India, we find that the epicentre of Christianity is moving city ward. This trend, more evident in the last thirty years or so, was reported in the 1981 Census of India.[7] India has a growing number of Christians living in cities and they must be informed and equipped to engage effectively in ministry and mission to the urban population. There is woeful lack of theological analysis and reflection on what is happening in cities. Mere sociological analysis will not suffice; the city has to be skilled in exegesis as well. The pace of urbanisation is so rapid, the urgency of the task so pressing and the complexity of the context so challenging that we are tempted to move in multiple directions without informed theological reflection and action. Looking at the city from the perspective of the Church, which is apparently weak and divided, also adds to these complexities.

**Illustrative Views**

The biblical account of the city exhibits amazing contrasts and dichotomies. On the one hand, cities are portrayed as symbols of human arrogance, pride and self-sufficiency and on the other, cities are also a manifestation of human capacity for creativity implanted in human beings by God.

---

[5] Prakas V. L. S. Rao, *Urbanisation in India: Spatial Dimensions,* New Delhi: Concept Publishing Company, 1983, p. 53.

[6] Donald Bogue and K. C. Zachariah, 'Urbanisation and Migration in India' in Roy Turner (ed.), *India's Urban Future,* Berkley: University of California Press, 1962, p 27.

[7] *Census of India* Series-1, Paper 4 of 1984: Household Population by Religion of Head of Household, Mumbai: Government Press, 1984.

Broadly three views illustrate the prevailing position to cities, which invariably influences urban mission. The first view condemns cities as downright evil; Jacques Ellul is a representative of this view. In his classic book *The Meaning of the City*[8] he has assumed a very pessimistic posture to cities; seeing them as the ultimate expression of humanity's rejection of God. Cain, a murderer, built the first city; the city is inherently evil. Real hope is possible only with the coming of the New Jerusalem.

The second view portrays the city as good. Harvey Cox in his book entitled, *The Secular City*, provides a second reading of the city and presents a case for urbanisation not being feared. Cox agrees with Wayne Meeks that urbanisation facilitated the spread of Christianity in the early church.[9] Secularisation, as opposed to the philosophy of secularism, opens the door for the church to shed its non-traditional approaches and engage in meaningful social ministries. This view strongly contends that the city is a manifestation of Christian life and faith, not antagonistic to it nor to be deplored and despised.

The third view maintains that the city is both good and evil. Robert Linthicum in his book entitled, *City of God, City of Satan*, asserts that the city is neither essentially good nor evil, but rather an arena of war. Satan desires to use the city and its systems and structures for his own purposes.

**Urban Mission**
The urban mission must deal with realities of the life of humanity and help understand what God is doing in movements and changes taking place everywhere. This is possible through the presence of the Holy Spirit in the Church and in the life of the believer, which causes him to trust the creative and providential power of the Father to direct all things towards the glorifying of the Son. God's particular focus on the Church has as its purpose the blessing of the nations (Gen. 12:1-3, 15; 17; Isa. 42:6). The Church is called to exist for the sake of its Lord and for the sake of humankind (Matt. 22:32-40).

---

[8] Jacques Ellul, *The Meaning of the City*, Grand Rapids: Eerdmans, 1970.

[9] W. A. Meeks, *The First Urban Christian: The Social World of the Apostle Paul*, New Haven: Yale University Press, 1983, p. 25.

A constructive engagement with the issues that impact the urban mission of the Church requires an understanding of the nature and work of the Triune God as Father, Son and Holy Spirit. Mission is at the heart of the trinitarian life of God. "Because God is triune, God can bless us. Because God blesses the other in God, God can bless the other without. Because God reaches out to another already within, God is not contained by the trinity's inner life, but can reach out also to us."[10] And precisely because Christians participate in the life of God, mission is at the heart of the Church. The Church is called to live the trinitarian faith as God has it for us. Trinitarian theology illustrates not only the internal life of God, but also the relationship between God and the Church, human society and all creation in which history and eschatology play a central role.

Whilst we must avoid the trap of insisting that everything is mission—for then, as Stephen Neill has reminded us, "nothing is mission"[11]—the church is perhaps in more risk of delineating mission too narrowly than too widely. We would do well to heed the words of Bosch, who describes mission as "a multifaceted ministry, in respect of witness, service, justice, healing, reconciliation, liberation, peace, evangelism, fellowship, church planting, contextualization, and much more."[12] In order to participate in that mission, we need courage to look beyond our ecclesiological boundaries and wisdom to discern where the Spirit is at work, often in the unlikeliest places and in the most improbable ways. In the mission context, the community of faith in its outward orientation embraces the neighbour, stranger and outcast.

God has called the Church to proclaim the Gospel (evangel) in word and deed. The term 'Gospel' in the New Testament is clear and precise: The gospel is the good news of God's redemptive act revealed in history

---

[10] Rogers, Eugene F., Jr., "The Stranger as Blessing" in Buckley and Yeago (eds.), *Knowing the Triune God: The Work of the Spirit in the Practices of the Church*, Grand Rapids; Eerdmans, 2001. p. 271.

[11] Stephen Neill, *Creative Tension*, London: Edinburgh House Press, 1959: 81.

[12] David J Bosch., *Transforming Mission: Paradigm Shifts in Theology of Mission*, Maryknoll: Orbis Books, 1991:512.

through the mediatorial life and work of Jesus Christ. At the centre is the resurrection of the crucified Jesus, who was sacrificed for our sins. It is this gospel that has been handed down and announced from generation to generation, as made clear by the Apostle Paul in 1 Corinthians 15:3-5: "For I delivered to you as of first importance what I also received: that Christ died for our sins in accordance with the Scriptures, that he was buried, that he was raised on the third day in accordance with the Scriptures, and that he appeared to Cephas, then to the twelve." The New Testament unveils the gospel's central event: the eternal Word became flesh, God's "only begotten Son" (John 1:14, 18), Jesus of Nazareth by name. We are used to understanding God's action in Christ in history as distinct, separate event and thus we develop a doctrine of incarnation, redemption, resurrection, exaltation and a doctrine of the Second Coming. It is proper to view the various dimensions of the Christological event, from the incarnation through the Second Coming, as interconnected aspects of one multifaceted jewel.

Father Matta El Meskeen of the Coptic Orthodox Church aptly describes the cross of Christ as the greatest manifestation of the missional movement of God, in so far as visible events are concerned, for in it God was crucified for humans. We know without a shadow of doubt that the cross is suffering in its greatest, most oppressive and unjust form. "We must also sense that the cross is, so to speak, the beast of burden upon which God Almighty rode to descend from his dwelling place, where he had been veiled from all eternity, and come to us and take us by the hand. The cross is the supreme power of the dynamism of God, which brought God down to us and clearly revealed him."[13] At the heart of the Gospel is the fact as Paul states, "God was reconciling the world to himself in Christ" (2 Cor. 5:19).

The Gospel is the life-giving medicine, spreading the fragrance of the knowledge of God revealed in Jesus Christ, calling women and men to share in the life of God. In Christ is the remedy for a life of joyful victory, over all forms of enslavement to evil, for a vibrant relationship

---

[13] Fr. Matta El-Meskeen, *The Passion of Jesus Christ in our Life,* Cairo: The Monastery of St Macarius, 2002, p. 17.

with God and one another. The atoning sacrifice and victorious resurrection of Christ and the indwelling Holy Spirit causes our frail lives to become the aroma of Christ to God (2 Cor. 2:14-15).

What then are the challenges for urban mission and how do we address them?

## Challenges for Urban Mission

The process of urbanisation presents innumerable challenges for urban Mission:

### *Passionate Youngsters*

India is a nation of young people. Around 47 per cent of India's current 1.2 billion people are under the age of 20, and teenagers among them number about 160 million. The Church sometimes is unnerved by the passionate youth of the cities. However, as James Loder recognised, there lies within adolescent passion a redemptive opening for the gospel. He taught that teenage passion is the key that unlocks adolescent struggle for meaning and purpose. Adolescents seek something, someone "to die for," to use the slang of young people, someone beyond themselves who "grabs" them because this someone alone is worthy of their love, their dedication and indeed the glad surrender of their entire life. The passion of Christ, as popularised by the Hollywood motion picture, is good news to adolescents not because Jesus suffers, but because Jesus loves so extravagantly, with such self-giving abandon, that young people find themselves and their communities transformed in and through the story of God's pathos revealed in Jesus' life, death and resurrection. "The *pathos* of God turns human passion inside out—redeeming, redirecting and reconstituting it according to the dimensions of Christ's self-giving love."[14]

---

[14] Dana R. Wright with Kenda Creasy Dean, ""Youth Passion, and Intimacy in the Context of Koinonia" James E. Loder's Contributions to a Practical Theology of imitation Christi for youth Ministry" in Dana R. Wright, and John D.Kuentzel (eds.), *Redemptive Transformation in Practical Theology*, Michigan: William B. Eerdmans, 2004, pp153-188.

The teenagers and young in the city lack role models in people of integrity. Questions of truth and authenticity are real issues for youth and they consider these as real alternates to socialised distortions presented by society. The youth are also under tremendous pressure to conform to the patterns of older generations. Adolescent passion is neither a "modern disease" nor a "barbarian invasion," as claimed by various theorists.[15] Most youngsters do not give up their passion for ultimate meaning without a fight. One way in which the youth fights conformity to the Church is by leaving spiritually domesticated congregations and joining new congregations where newer expressions of Christian spirituality make them feel at home.

Teens tend to perceive themselves in a kind of "lost" state between the fading glory of childhood and the terrifying emptiness and awful meaninglessness of the adult "world" stretched out in front of them, expressing itself in a sense of loneliness, isolation and cynicism. Youth often masquerade as being adults. The good news is that God has filled the void with the life-giving power of God's presence through which adolescents find abundant life in the Spirit. Christ makes the person a new creation by engrafting the person through the Spirit into Christ's body, justifying, sanctifying and calling according to the initiative of God revealed in the cross. It is our duty to communicate to the young people that their own identity and their relations with others is God's radical gift.

A majority of young people give in to cultural pressures to conform. Poor self-esteem, unhealthy social relationships and exposure to suicide on television are the main reasons for the growing trend of suicide in the city. There has been a rapid increase in the number of affluent youth taking to crime, robbery, kidnapping and extortion in order to fund their wasteful lifestyles.

---

[15] On adolescence as "disease", see Douglas Foster, "The years of Living Dangerously," *Rolling Stone 71* (December 9, 1993):55. On adolescence as a "barbarian invasion", see the reference to Talcott Parsons in Loder, *The logic of the Spirit, human development in theological perspective,* San Francisco: Josey-Bass Publishers. p.204.

With the impact of globalisation on the middle class in India, religion has become more a matter of ritual than a spiritual experience.[16] Spirituality is perhaps a means to cope with stress, be it physical, emotional or mental that comes with ambition. Youth today see religion as an anchor as well as identity.[17]

Over 250 youngsters, including 29 girls and 12 foreign nationals, were arrested for having a rave party with drugs in Pune.[18] Watching porn and experimenting with drugs and alcohol are also common among teenagers.

The Church in urban mission must proclaim and model that the grace of God in Jesus Christ by the power of the Holy Spirit working in us transforms the human ego, setting it free from the underlying feeling of being lost. This is further made clear when we consider that the incarnation of Jesus Christ has two constitutive aspects, condescension and accommodation. In incarnation, Jesus accommodated human nature, transformed it and restored it to its origin in God. Christ has already overcome the barriers to communion and human effort since all other grounds will always fall short of redemptive transformation. Therefore, the Church congregations that hand over their youth to be groomed by the unredeemed social influences grieve the Spirit. The fellowship (*Koinonia*) is constituted only by the Spirit's transforming work in a dynamic relation with the Triune God and one another.

The youth will continue to demand that congregations embody the life of Christ. If they do not find the real thing in congregations, teens in particular will continue to act out in violent, anti-social behaviour. They will conform to the "plastic worlds" of false imitation we have created, or destroy themselves looking for love in all the wrong places. "The youth will not darken the door of a passionless Church in which

---

[16] C. Sarat Chandran, 'The Reform Agents', *The New Sunday Express Magazine*, 9 March 2008, p. 2.

[17] Prerna Uppal, 'The Divine Youth', *The Week*, 6 July 2008, p. 36–44.

[18] 'Police Raid Pune Rave Party,' http://timesofindia.indiatimes.com/articleshow/1722702.cms accessed on 4 March 2007.

the imitation of Christ looks suspiciously more like imitation of the form culture than of the life of Christ."[19] Young and old people alike would give anything to be part of a community that loved as passionately as Jesus did. Sadly, for many youth love is an alien concept.

## *Human Trafficking*

India is a source, destination and transit country for men, women and children trafficked for the purposes of forced labour, commercial sexual exploitation and even for the sale of human organs. No confirmed data is available, but NGOs estimate this problem affects 20 to 65 million Indians. Women and girls are trafficked and forced to marry especially in those areas where the sex ratio is highly skewed in favour of men.

In India about 45,000 children are trafficked every year; most of them remain untraceable. In Delhi, a child goes missing every hour and 20 children are abducted every day. In Mumbai, 4,297 children went missing in 2006 and 3,748 in 2007.[20] Children are subjected to forced labour as factory workers, domestic servants, beggars and agriculture workers and have been used as armed combatants by some terrorist and insurgent groups. The Internet has become a new exploiter of children. Thousands of sexually explicit and exploitative material of children, sometimes as young as 6 or 7, is uploaded to the Internet.[21]

The urgent need is to mobilise and sensitise the Church to address issues of negligence, exploitation and discrimination against the poor, the dalits, tribal children and other children at risk in India. This would involve building the Church's capacity and strengthening its involvement in advocating, promoting and securing the rights of children and networking with government agencies and like-minded NGOs to build and support existing network within the communities.

---

[19] Dana R. Wright with Kenda Creasy Dean, "Youth Passion, and Intimacy in the Context of Koinonia" p.186

[20] Ajay Uprety, "Where Are Our Kids?' *The Week*, 19 July 2009, p.18–22.

[21] Mohuya Chaudhuri, 'Child Pornography on Social Networking Websites,' *http://www.ndtv.com/convergence/ndtv/story*.

## Oppression of Women

The Church has often failed to teach and practice that both male and female are equally created in the image and likeness of God (Gen. 1:27) and that Jesus Christ by his sacrificial death equally redeemed both male and female (1 Cor. 15: 3-4). In addition, the gifts of the Holy Spirit are equally given to men and women (1 Cor. 1:7). The Church in mission should be in the forefront of modelling equality.

Domestic violence darkens the doors of Christian homes. Today, women place their faith in pepper spray, rather than karate and knives, for self-defence.[22] A UN report indicates that approximately 200 girls (160 plus are coerced) and women in India enter sex work every day. India has nearly 2.5 million prostitutes in nearly 300,000 brothels in 1,100 red-light areas across the country. Despite the Pre-Natal Diagnostics Test Act 1994, 900,000 unborn girl children are aborted in India each year. [23] Crime against women has increased, from 7.4 per cent of the total in 2002 to 8.2 per cent during 2006, with Delhi leading in crime. India reported 34,175 molestation cases in 2005. The number increased to 36,617 in 2006. Many tourists, too, have fallen prey to crimes committed by Indians. One estimate says a woman is raped every 32 minutes, murdered every 22 minutes and molested every 15 minutes in India.[24] The community of faith should repent of its evil, model mutuality and create structures of support for suffering women.

## Family in Crisis

The sanctity of married life and the understanding of family as a marriage between man and woman as taught in the Bible is under attack as some leaders approve of gay marriages. Live-in relationships are common in

---

[22] 'Pepper Spray to Women's Aid, Sales Reach All Time High,' http://timesofindia.indiatimes.com/Cities/Pepper-spray-to-womens-aid-Sales-Reach-All-time-High/articleshow/4328857.cms accessed on 29 March 2009.

[23] Neha Dixit, 'The Nowhere Children,' *Tehelka*, 1 November 2008, p.28–42.

[24] Parikshit Luthra, 'Crime against Women on the Upswing, Says Figures,' http://www.ibnlive.com/news/crimes-against-women-on-the-upswing-say-figures/55485-3.html accessed on 7 March 2008.

cities like Bangalore now.[25] Between January and June 2009, as many as 1,400 couples in Bangalore city filed for divorce in family courts. There is an average of 25 cases of matrimonial discord being filed every day.[26] For every five weddings registered in Mumbai and Thane since 2002, family courts have received two applications for divorce. Exactly 104,287 marriages were registered in Mumbai and Thane between January 2002 and October 2007. During the same period, the family courts in the two districts received 44,922 applications for divorce.[27] On average, one child is disowned by its parents each day in Delhi. A leading magazine reported that extramarital affairs find justification in religion. Men indulging in extramarital affairs claim to arouse the Krishna in them and the women, Radha. In cities, divorce is accepted as a way of life and as nothing extraordinary.[28]

Family life is one area where the Church must take lead in modelling the love of Christ for his Church. As the Bible teaches, "Husbands love your wives, just as Christ loved the Church and gave himself up for her" (Eph. 5:25). Both men and women work side by side; a good example of this is the role of Mary and Joseph.

## *Pollution*

Indian cities face air, water and noise pollution and pollution due to improper sewage and waste management systems. Health hazards are created by air pollution, bringing down the quality of life and leaving people feeling ill and tired in the city of Delhi. One in 10 people have asthma in Delhi, which has 4 million registered vehicles.[29] The country's

---

[25] Rakshita Adyanthaya, 'Marriages Not Quite Made in Heaven,' http://expressbuzz.com/edition/story.aspx?.

[26] '25 Divorce Cases Filed Every Day,' *http://timesofindia.indiatimes.com*

[27] '2 Divorces for Every 5 Marriages in Mumbai,' *http://timesofindia.indiatimes.com/2_divorces_for_every_5_marriages_in_Mumbai/articleshow/2729438.cms* accessed on 25th January 2008.

[28] Anita Jain, *Marrying Anita,* London: Bloomsbury Publishing Plc, 2008, p. 189.

[29] Sanchita Sharma, 'SOS! Delhi's Polluted Air Is Killing People,' http://www.hindustantimes.com/StoryPage/StoryPage.aspx?id=eda7a8ba-94f5-410bbdbbdb2c9edc27c3&MatchID1=4625&TeamID1=1&TeamID2=6&MatchType1=1&SeriesID1=116

financial capital, Mumbai, has recently been branded seventh in a list of the world's dirtiest cities in a report compiled by *Forbes* Magazine.[30] Since God created this world and made us stewards of his beautiful creation and believing that God supports human life universally, we should not pollute our environment or waste our earth's resources. We must be unequivocally pro-human life. Like our God we must be known for our kindness to persons as persons.

## *Slum Dwellers*

Among the urban poor, slum dwellers are the poorest. A slum, as defined by the United Nations agency UN-Habitat, is a run-down area of a city characterised by substandard housing and filth and lacking in residence security. According to the United Nations, the percentage of urban dwellers living in slums decreased from 47 per cent to 37 per cent in the developing world between 1990 and 2005.[31] However, due to the rising population and the rise especially in urban populations, the number of slum dwellers is rising. One billion people worldwide live in slums.[32] This figure is likely grow to 2 billion by 2030.[33]

The very definition of slum points at the acute drinking water and sanitation crisis for slum dwellers. Within India, for an area to be recognised as a slum, it should be a cluster located within an urban area without proper access to water and sanitation. As per the 2001 census of India, 640 towns spread over 26 states and union territories have reported existence of slums. This means one out of every four persons reside in slums in our cities and towns. The NSSO survey in 2002 has identified

---

*5&MatchID2=4629&TeamID3=5&TeamID4=10&MatchType2=2&SeriesID2=1 166&PrimaryID=4625&Headline=SOS!+Delhi%e2%80%99s+polluted+air+ is+killing+people* assessed on 26th December 2007.

[30] Sowmya Katathil, 'Forbes Magazine Names Mumbai as City of Junk,' *http:/ /www.ndtv.com/convergence/ndtv/story.aspx?id=NEWEN20080043169&ch=3/6/ 2008%203:10:00%20PM* accessed on 6th March 2008.

[31] http://www.un.org/millenniumgoals/pdf/mdg2007.pdf p. 26.

[32] Mike Davis, *Planet of Slums* London, New York 2006.

[33] Slum Dwellers to double by 2030 UN-HABITAT report, April 2007.

51,688 slums in urban areas of which 50.6 per cent of urban slums have been declared as 'notified slums.' This growing slum population and the lack of basic facilities will badly impact on India's overall target achievement in the water and sanitation sector.

Since 1972 the Government of India initiated a programme called Environmental Improvement of Urban Slums under which priority to drinking water and sanitation was given. Again in 1996, the government initiated the National Slum Development Programme with substantial fund allocation. It had a specified focus on providing drinking water and community toilets. After spending close to Rs. 3,100 crores in nine years, it was discontinued. It was estimated that 46 million slum dwellers benefited from it.

In 2005, the government started Jawaharlal Nehru Urban Renewal Mission, an initiative to encourage reforms and fast-track planned development of certain cities. It has a financial commitment of Rs.1,50,000 crores during 2006-12. The larger objective of the mission is to integrate development of infrastructure services, accelerate the flow of investment into urban infrastructure services; planned development of cities including semi-urban areas and universalisation of urban services to ensure their availability to the urban poor.

Mumbai has the highest number of people living in slums with 6.4 million. Delhi has 1.85 million and Kolkata 1.48 million people living in slums. The majority of Indians have less than 10-by-10-foot room for their living, sleeping, cooking, washing and toilet needs. Besides, 32 per cent of urban houses are 258 square feet or less in area. Given the fact that urban households have an average size of 4.3 persons, this translates to 60 square feet per person, which is exactly the minimum specified for US prisons.[34]

God cares passionately for the issues of poverty and justice. A concern for the poor and an emphasis on just and fair behaviour flows like a river through the Bible. What does it mean to worship God? Singing songs in

---

[34] Atul Thakur, '1/3 of India Lives in Houses Smaller Than US Jail Cells,' *The Times of India*, 25 November 2008, p.1.

the Church or sharing food with the hungry? It is not "either/or," but "both/and." God calls people to worship him through bringing liberty to the oppressed, feeding the starving and clothing the naked. God wants lives of restorative worship; restoration means more than pasting a sticking plaster on the wound. The society pictured by Isaiah had not been 'patched up.' Instead, there is wholeness on permanent change, on bringing people back into wholeness and health. This is what Isaiah spoke on behalf of God:

> Is not this the fast that I choose: to loose the bonds of wickedness, to undo the straps of the yoke, to let the oppressed go free, and to break every yoke? Is it not to share your bread with the hungry and bring the homeless poor into your house; when you see the naked, to cover him, and not to hide yourself from your own flesh? Then shall your light break forth like the dawn, and your healing shall spring up speedily; your righteousness shall go before you; the glory of the Lord shall be your rear guard. Then you shall call, and the Lord will answer; you shall cry, and he will say, 'Here I am.' If you take away the yoke from your midst, the pointing of the finger, and speaking wickedness, if you pour yourself out for the hungry and satisfy the desire of the afflicted, then shall your light rise in the darkness and your gloom be as the noonday. And the Lord will guide you continually and satisfy your desire in scorched places and make your bones strong; and you shall be like a watered garden, like a spring of water, whose waters do not fail. And your ancient ruins shall be rebuilt; you shall raise up the foundations of many generations; you shall be called the repairer of the breach, the restorer of streets to dwell in.
>
> Isaiah 58:6-12

Changing the life of the homeless implies more than temporary solutions, more than a bed for night. It means looking at education, employment, security, health, deeper issues, but ones that makes lasting changes. "So, not just a patch of land, but a well-watered garden. Not just a roof over someone's head, but a home. Not just the absence of war but restorative, healing peace." [35]

---

[35] Poverty and Justice Bible, The British and Foreign Bible Society 1997, Notes p.27.

## Free Market Economy

In our journey of transformation in this world, the household of Christ and market society are uncomfortable partners. The basic goal of market society to transform is to help cope with a new, more challenging competitive free market environment of economic globalisation. Economic globalisation promotes the culture of consumerist individualism and accelerates the massive shift of economic opportunity, resources and wealth to the existing multinational corporate giants of power. Capitalists make profits on their investments. Have you stopped to ponder if you like the existing dictatorship of money and organisational tyranny?

Globalisation involves a worldview; it narrates a story in which the universal dominance of unfettered capitalism is irresistible and beneficent. For the capitalist, every part of life becomes a commodity, something to be bought and sold, whether it is a computer, the latest automobile, sporting, technological skills, sex or our ability to work. It is assumed, apparently, that we are in the clutch of the determination of economic laws considered as laws of the universe. It is painfully discouraging to see economics elevated to the position of ultimate justifier and explainer of all affairs of daily life and competition enshrined as the sovereign principle and ideal of economics.

Competition always involves, and in fact requires, that community must be divided into classes of winners and losers, as if this justifies everything and anything. Competition results in unlimited concentration of economic power in the hands of a few.

The reality of market is all-encompassing as its channels flow into every nation, city and village of the world. Even though market is changing the world, it will not redeem the world. The market has no power against sin, evil and death despite its claims of universal spread and effectiveness. According to Robert Heilbroner, the nature of our society is accumulation of wealth as power and the logic of our society is exchange of commodities.[36] Everything hops around these realities. Modern people

---

[36] Heilbroner, Robert, *The Nature and Logic of Capitalism*, New York: W.W. Norton, 1985, pp.31-32.

believe in them implicitly and shape their lives according to this logic. It is increasingly the reason through which people expect life, happiness, security and future. No one can deny its awesome effect on modernity.

The revolution that began with machines and chemicals proposes now to continue with mechanisation, computers and biotechnology. In the information-based modern economic society, the individual comes up against an ever faster circulation of goods, images, money, ideas and other human beings. The shared meanings and healthy practices of community are emptied out in the process of isolation of the self. The rare product of modernity is the isolated individual in the midst of technological society, yet embedded in relationships that transcend time and space, via mobile phone and the worldwide Internet.

## *Education Institutions*

The institutions of learning give themselves to a hysterical rhetoric of 'change,' 'the future,' 'the frontiers of modern science,' 'competition,' 'the competitive edge,' 'the cutting edge,' 'early adoption' and the like, as if there is nothing worth learning from the past and nothing worth preserving in the present. Teachers and scholars are expected to develop "human capital" and impart economic advantage rather than pass on a common cultural heritage. The ambition is to make university an 'economic resource' in a competition for wealth and power that is local, national and global. One cannot maintain one's 'competitive edge' if one helps other people. The advantage of 'early adoption' would disappear; it would not be thought of within a community that put proper value on mutual help. Such advantages would not be considered by people intent on loving their neighbours as themselves.

The proponents of competition never tire of repeating that their work has been done and is still being done under the heading of altruism (unselfishness). For example, in agriculture, the constant slogan is 'serve agriculture' and 'feed the world.' As previously stated, these aims are irreproachable. However, these aims raise a number of doubts. Agriculture, it turns out, is to be served strictly according to the rules of competitive economics. The aim is to make farmers and Indian agriculture more competitive. With whom, we must ask, are our farmers and agriculture competitive? And we must say: Against other farmers, at home and abroad.

The question we finally come to is a practical one. Can a university or nation afford this exclusive rule of competition, this purely economic economy? The great fault of this approach is its drastically reductive nature; it does not permit us to live and work as human beings, as the best of our inheritance defines us. Rats live by competition under the law of supply and demand; it is the privilege of human beings to live under the laws of justice and compassion. It is impossible to not notice how little the proponents of the ideal of competition have to say about honesty, the fundamental economic virtue, and how very little they have to say about community, compassion and mutual help.

## *Communal Riots*

Animals fight but they do not wage wars. Humans are the only creatures who pursue enthusiastically mass killing of their own kind in a planned manner. The oldest traditions of humanity, its myth and epic poetry, speak primarily of killings.

Daring shootouts, gang wars and criminals roaming in the open with sophisticated foreign-made firearms and country-made pistols have made cities unsafe for citizens. In God's fallen world, history narrates a gory tale of pursuit and misuse of absolute power and control that dominates and decimates humans. The ruthless market economy celebrates accumulation of wealth as power, even by crushing its competitors, leaving behind a trail of casualties of crippled losers. Race-based narratives of social structures seem to suggest that consequent racial differences produce inherent superiority of a particular race. The discourse of casteism has exploited and divided humans for thousands of years through categories of purity and pollution. Even human rights activists, who fight for justice, divide humans as oppressors and oppressed.

However, there is good news for humans in conflict. Reconciliation is God's gift; it does not begin with our activism or condition. The fifth chapter of 2 Corinthians offers a beautiful and radical vision: God's "new creation" in Christ and our becoming his ambassadors of reconciliation (vv. 17-21).

How then should Christians respond to situations of communal riots in India? Between 1950 and 1995, Mumbai had the shady distinction of having the most number of riots and riot-related deaths. Suresh Khopade analysed the causes of riots in Mumbai and Bhiwandi and success in insuring peace. He said, "After the Ayodhya incident the city of Mumbai burned twice but the notoriously communally hypersensitive town of Bhiwandi, remained completely calm. Not a stone thrown there. Experts from all over the nation and the world descended upon Bhiwandi to study this miracle."[37] Khopade admits that undercurrents are very strong due to the scars left by earlier riots, the biases and history. His research proved that the Peace Committee set up by the Home Department did not help in maintaining peace. "The members of the peace committee itself make speeches in villages instigating communal hatred and tension."[38]

When Khopade interviewed the poor victims of riots, "Tulsi, whose son was hacked to death before her eyes, hit her forehead and gave the typical reply of a Hindu woman. 'Sir, it was my karma-what else?'"[39] Chandni, whose husband was killed, "raised her eyes and hands, palms up, towards the sky and said, 'What can I say sir? This was the will of Allah!'" [40] What sort of response is required from the follower of Christ?

Khopade formed a Mohalla Committee in each municipal ward. Every area where Hindu-Muslim conflicts had taken place had about 70 Mohalla Committees, which included a minimum of 50 Muslim and 50 Hindus along with police officers and members of civil societies. These handled all non-cognizable cases and applications were brought before the Mohalla Committee for resolution.[41] The efforts of Khopade resulted in transformation from endemic violence to peace.

---

[37] Suresh Khopade, *Why Mumbai Burned ...and Bhiwandi Did Not*, Pune: Sangram Khopade, 2010, p.25.

[38] *Ibid.*, p. 37.

[39] *Ibid.*, p.33.

[40] *Ibid.*, p.33.

[41] *Ibid.*, The details of formation and functions of Mohalla Committee are given on pages 38 and 39.

The Church in mission is duty bound to promote peace in society, even though Christians from all denominations have suffered at the hands of militant factions of the Sangh Parivar. After the death of Swami Laxmananda Saraswati at the hands of the Maoists, on 23 August 2008, Sangh Parivar workers unleashed violence against Christians for 42 days, killing nearly 100 people, burning 147 churches, leaving nearly 48,000 people homeless and raping a nun. The state government completely failed in its duty to protect innocent Christians who were unable to defend themselves. The police stood by and occasionally joined the Sangh mobs in the violence. The atrocities against the Christians in Orissa were the worst ever in the recorded history of Christianity in India.

The story is the same in Karnataka. The state was under an unprecedented wave of Christian persecution, having faced more than 1,000 attacks in 500 days. On 26 January 2010, the day we celebrated India's Republic Day, Karnataka's 1000th attack took place in Mysore city. In the past few years, the number of attacks on Christians, recorded by the Evangelical Fellowship of India, has been more than 1,000 attacks a year. The Freedom of Religion Bill in seven states of India requires an individual to take permission from the designated government officers before deciding to worship Christ and becoming his follower.

The Christian community in India does not have a history of involvement in religious violence, even though we are victims of violence. They work to alleviate human misery and injustice because they believe God loves all people equally and desires justice for all. We journey together with Jesus Christ in the midst of a world of injustice, deception and violence in order to rescue those in bondage.

## *Suffering as Part of Christian Identity*

The Church must integrate suffering and pain as part of the Church's life story. The overwhelming biblical language for mission and promoting faith reflects the notion of blessing rather than warfare, reconciliation and peace rather than violence and hatred. Those traumatised and wounded by violence require healing of their memories. How should the Church remember and respond to suffering, persecution and martyrdom? Should we harbour cold and enduring anger and thirst for revenge and react like a wounded animal? In order to respond as free human beings, we must value feelings, even the desire for revenge. However, we must also follow moral requirements implanted by God into the framework of our humanity. As the Church, we must be determined to not lose sight of the command to love our neighbour, even if the other acts as our enemy. The victim might question, "Shouldn't the perpetrators who are truly guilty be dealt with as they deserve to be treated with the strict enforcement of retributive justice?" The State is a gift of God's common grace and is granted authority to maintain law and order and restrain evil in society (Rom 13:1-7). However, it needs to be highlighted that Christian love of the enemy does not exclude the concerns for justice but goes beyond it, to forgiveness and reconciliation. "Violence is not human destiny because the God of peace is the beginning and the end of human history. God can create a world of justice, truth, and peace only by making an end to deception, injustice, and violence. The end of the world is not violence, but a nonviolent embrace without end."[42]

## Transformational Engagement

Leadership in government and business is often equated with the creation of wealth and prosperity, increasing the price of share, growing the economy, but the Bible calls for creation of justice. Who's your master? Is it God or money, people or possessions? We live divided lives. We know where our heart should be—it should be in serving God, but so often we spend more time and devotion on our other master—money. The Bible is realistic. We need money to live. People need to earn a living. But there is a difference between earning money and worshipping it. We need to master money before it masters us.

True Christian spirituality works from inside out. What you believe is expressed in what you do. This involves the transformation of our lives. Transformation is the change from a condition of human existence contrary to God's purposes to one in which people are able to enjoy fullness of life in harmony with God.

---

[42] Volf, Miroslav, *Exclusion and Embrace*, Nashville: Abingdon Press 1996, p.300.

Transformation is a concept rooted in the New Covenant (see John 4:14; Rom. 12:2; II Cor. 3:18, 5:17; I John 3:9). The term itself derives from the Greek word 'metamorphosis', which means to change from one degree of glory to another with ever-increasing glory. It is the spiritual equivalent of a caterpillar being metamorphosed into a butterfly. Unlike reformation, it does not merely fiddle with society; it changes it from the inside out. It operates at the heart level. Transformation is the progressive and ongoing measurable supernatural impact of the presence and power of God working in, through and apart from the Church on human society and structures. In the Church, this is characterised by increased holiness of life, reconciliation in relationships and appetite for prayer and worship. Through the Church this is characterised by proclamation of the gospel, mobilisation of gifts and callings and an increased relevance to and participation in greater society on issues of compassion and justice.

In culture, this may be characterised by pervasive awareness of the reality of God, a radical correction of social ills, a commensurate decrease in crime rates, supernatural blessing on local commerce, healing of the alienated and disenfranchised, regenerative acts of restoring the productivity of the land and an exporting of kingdom righteousness.

The urban church must work in a spirit of co-operation, resulting in healthy churches in every class and kind of people and within practical and relational reach of every person, permeating every segment of society with the love, truth and saving power of Jesus Christ.

The urban churches' transformational development of the poor through community development programmes will create a better future for the poor. Poverty is a set of disempowering systems. There is the biophysical system—body and mind—which represents the basic human needs of health and education. There is the cultural system in terms of inadequacies in worldview. There is the captivity promoting anti-life and deception through religious systems. These systems interact and contribute to the disempowerment and marred identity of the urban poor living in slums.

Urban transformational mission involves seeking positive change in the whole of human life, materially, socially and spiritually, by recovering our true identity as human beings created in the image of God and discovering our true vocation as productive stewards, faithfully caring for our world and people.

## Chapter 9

# Feminist Perspectives in Mission

## Bernadette O Connell Beville

> And afterwards I will pour out my Spirit on all people, Your sons and daughters will prophesy...
>
> Joel 2:28
>
> Even on my servants, both men and women, I will pour out my spirit in those days...
>
> Acts 2:18[1]

The verses quoted above are favourite verses of feminists of faith. They encapsulate the hope and events that the Gospel brings as foretold by Joel and echoed in Acts. It restores both men and women to the precious place of collaborative ministry and service to God that was initiated in Genesis and that was damaged as a consequence of the Fall. We are told, in the West, that the present era, in which we live, is both post-Christian and post-feminist. A sign of the post-feminist era is a generation of young women who are now growing up taking for granted what was painstakingly wrought for them by their foremothers and seeing a world of equal opportunity before them.

---

[1] New International Version, USA: Zondervan, 1986.

However, in reality, all is not as it seems, although some may be weary of hearing of women's rights, feminist issues and gender topics; nevertheless, there is much to be done by and for women both in secular society and within the church in these matters. In fact, this cynical attitude only re-emphasises the importance of the feminist task of critiquing the past from a feminist point of view, rediscovering the history of women and reconstructing feminist knowledge, and these are paralleled in Christian feminism. As Ann Carr says of the Christian feminist agenda:

> The first task is to critique the past from the point of view of feminist experience. The second is to rediscover the history of Christian women...The third task is to reconstruct a Christian theology and the categories by which theology is done so that they include women's experience and wisdom.[2]

Much has been done and is still being done in critiquing the past from a feminist experience and thankfully the history of Christian women is being recovered and faithfully recorded[3] and in particular since the 1960s. We continue to have much to learn from the way God has called women to His service in the past. Reflecting on the extraordinary things He did in women's lives and in women's ministries can raise our expectations and open our minds and hearts to what God can do and indeed is doing in these days. This is good biblical practice and we see this pattern in the Old and New Testaments, as God's people look at their history and recall what God has done for them and his faithfulness to them; for example, Joshua Chapter 24 and Acts Chapter 13.

With regard to reconstructing a Christian theology that includes women, nowhere is this more significant than in the role of women in mission. By mission I am referring to the broader work of the church to which we are all called as believers, not just evangelism, but of course including evangelism and missionary work. This understanding of mission is outlined in the *New Dictionary of Theology*, where it says:

---

[2] Ann Carr, *Transforming Grace: Christian Tradition and Women's Experience*, San Francisco: Harper and Row, 1988.

[3] For example see: Narola Imchen, *Remembering our Foremothers*, Assam India: ETC, 2003 and *Women in the History of Christianity*, Assam: TDCC Publications:2010.

...every aspect of theology has an inescapably missiological dimension, for each one exists for the sake of the churches mission...In popular imagination mission is often misconceived as Christians crossing frontiers to spread the gospel. This view reflects a past age when Christians tended to divide the world neatly into Christian and non Christian. Today however, the missionary frontier runs around the world. It is the line which separates belief from unbelief. Mission takes place from and to all continents and within each nation.[4]

For women in the developing world (also known as the Third World) reconstructing theology involves "doing theology." As Ursula King says:[5]

It is theology as an activity, as an ongoing process rooted in praxis, interdependent with and compassionately committed to life, justice and freedom from oppression. It is not theology as a reified, academic subject with watertight categories, clear boundaries and sharp intellectual definitions totally separate from people's experience. Of course it includes a tremendous intellectual effort, much powerful and creative thinking, but this is life as lived, experienced, struggled through, wrestled with, and celebrated.

This means there are no sharp boundaries between women's voices coming out of the academic institutions and other women's voices speaking out in the community at large. There is a fluidity and continuity between the stories and reflections of all these women, a common participation in one another's experiences.

Indeed, as feminists of faith our experience of theology is not just dry and academic but also rooted in our experience. We in turn bring our experiences to the Lord, to the Scripture and there we are actively working through a theology that includes women as a central part of God's design. The Gospel of course brings great freedom and dignity to both men and women. We are privileged with our Gospel message from a compassionate, caring and loving God. We serve a Saviour who Himself is a model of servant leadership:

---

[4] Sinclair B. Ferguson, David F. Wright (eds.), [Cons. Ed. J.I. Packer]. *New Dictionary of Theology*, England: IVP 1988, 434/435.

[5] Ursula King, *Feminist Theology from the Third World: A Reader*, London: SPCK, 1994, 17.

Jesus declared himself as coming to serve not to be served and is the supreme example of servant leadership, he rejected the world's standards of leadership, he told his disciples in Matthew 20:26-27: Not so with you. Instead, whoever wants to become great among you must be your servant, and whoever wants to be first must be your slave – just as the Son of Man did not come to be served, but to serve, and to give his life as a ransom for many (NIV 1986).

For many Evangelical women, their desire is to serve their fellow believers, not necessarily 'lord it over' others. If the coming of Jesus brought in a new covenant and restoration after the Fall, it seems appropriate that women would be allowed full opportunity to use their gifting, graciously given to them by God.[6]

Since the rise of women's liberation in the 1960s, there has been an obvious development of a feminist critical consciousness[7] in secular society and within the church. Since this second wave of feminism, an understanding of feminism has developed that has become known as an evangelical egalitarian model.[8] This model sees male and female as created equally by God in Genesis and both given responsibility by God to work in mutually submissive roles of service without a need for hierarchy for the cause of the gospel and the glory of God. An acknowledgement that there is now neither male nor female in Christ is paramount to the future status and role of women in mission. In Galatians 3: 28-29, Paul writes:

> There is neither Jew nor Greek, slave nor free, male nor female, for you are all one in Christ Jesus. If you belong to Christ, then you are Abraham's seed, and heirs according to the promise (NIV 1986).

---

[6] B. O'Connell Beville, *Faith & Feminism,* thesis for MA in Women's Studies, UCC, 2010, 75.

[7] Sinclair B. Ferguson, David F. Wright (eds.), [Cons. Ed. J.I. Packer]. *New Dictionary of Theology*, England: IVP 1988, 255.

[8] For discussion of the complementarian model, etc., see: John Piper, Wayne Grudem, (eds.), *Recovering Biblical Manhood and Womanhood: A Response to Evangelical Feminism*, Illinois: Crossway Books, 1991. For discussion of the egalitarian model, etc., see: Ronald W. Pierce and Rebecca Merrill Grothuis, R. (Gen. Eds.) Gordon D. Fee (Contr. Ed.), *Discovering Biblical Equality: Complementarity without Hierarchy*, USA: Apollos/Intervarsity Press, 2005.

These verses declare unequivocally that men and women are one in Christ and that there is no distinction between the two. In response to these verses, John Stott in his commentary on Galatians says:

> This remarkable assertion of the equality of the sexes was made centuries in advance of the times. Women were nearly always despised in the ancient world, even in Judaism, and not infrequently exploited and ill-treated as well. But here the assertion is made that in Christ male and female are one and equal – and made by Paul, who is ignorantly supposed by many to have been anti-feminist.[9]

Stott identifies that Paul is clearly saying that now in Christ there is no distinction between male and female. He goes on to say that Paul, from a practical point of view, is not ignoring differences between the Jews and the Greeks, slaves and freemen, men and women; they do exist, but none of those differences change their status of equality in Christ. The Jews should not feel superior to the Greeks, anymore than men should not feel superior in any way to women.[10] We celebrate our differences as men and women and our uniqueness, as our Creator has made us, but these differences must not be used to subjugate, oppress or subordinate women either in the church or secular society.

It is essential therefore that the reconstruction of a theology of mission be cognizant of women's contribution from the past and become a catalyst for women's involvement going forward. The issues that are problematic for women and indeed as a consequence for men and children as well are at the heart of the church's mission. I summarise below the definition of the task of mission again as outlined in the *The New Dictionary of Theology*:

> 1. It [the church] is to be involved in stewarding the material resources of creation...renouncing greed...

> 2. It is to serve human beings without distinction and whatever their need. It has a compassionate task to aid refugees and the victims of drought and famine and to help set up development schemes, literacy campaigns, health education and housing programmes...

---

[9] John Stott, *The Message of Galatians*, Leicester: IVP 1988, 100.

[10] B. O'Connell Beville, *Faith & Feminism*, thesis for MA in Women's Studies, UCC, 2010, 78-79.

3. It must bear witness to "the truth as it is in Jesus...Bearing witness means both the verbal communication of...the gospel and the visual demonstration of its power to bring new life and hope to human relationships and communities...

4. It should engage to see that God's justice is done in society...defending family life against easy divorce, abortion,...pornography and the exploitation of women and children, and experimentation on early human life...seek alternatives to policies which give rise to more homeless, badly educated, undernourished and unemployed people. It will fight for human rights and against human discrimination...(especially racism). Finally it will challenge the inexorable build-up of weapons of mass destruction and the increasing arms trade between rich and poor nations...

5. It has a responsibility to show what it means in practice to be a reconciled and liberated community in the midst of a corrupt, distressed and despairing world. It is sent to demonstrate the reality of God's unmerited grace by practicing forgiveness, the sharing of goods and resources, by the elimination of prejudice and suspicion, and by exercising power as servanthood, not as domination and control...[11]

This task is indeed an enormous challenge to all of us. As believers, we must do more than just give mental or verbal adherence to such noble aspirations as outlined above. Again we are reminded here to model our use of resources and power on Jesus' model of leadership, as already mentioned above, a model of servanthood. We are urged in the gospel to live responsible lives; Jesus warns against ignoring the needs of those around us. In Matthew 25: 34-46, Jesus says the following familiar words:

> For I was hungry and you gave Me something to eat; I was thirsty and you gave Me to drink; I was a stranger and you invited Me in; naked and you clothed Me; I was sick, and you visited me; I was in prison and you came to me... 'Truly I say to you, to the extent that you did it to one of these brothers of mine, even the least of them, you did it to Me' (NAS 1992).[12]

As believers, we have the responsibility and the privilege to set about fulfilling the task that the Lord has given to his church, to bring good news to the poor, to tell prisoners they are set free, tell the blind they can

---

[11] Sinclair B. Ferguson, David F. Wright (eds.), [Cons. Ed. J.I. Packer], *New Dictionary of Theology*, England: IVP 1988, 434 – 436.

[12] New American Standard Version. CA., Foundation Press, 1992.

see and set free the downtrodden (Luke 4: 18). Women, however, some feminists argue, suffer from a double oppression, the general oppression in society (for example, lack of education, housing, possibilities of employment, violence, abuse and so on) and oppression and discrimination because of their gender. The statistics for the obstacles that many women face worldwide are available for all to consider. For example, feminist theology posits the view that women are the most oppressed in society:

> In our world women are the poorest and most oppressed by any indicators; in terms of health, education, economics, abuse and violence, whether by individuals or by social structures. In every country of the world men earn more pay for less work. It is estimated that women do 62% of the world's work hours, yet own only 1% of the world's property. Women form 75% of all sick people, 70% of all poor, 66% of illiterates and 80% of all refugees.[13]

These statistics are harrowing at the very least but we cannot ignore them. We are to be proactive in mission, proactive in our service, as women to the Lord, proactive in answering the call on our lives. We are called to be the voice of those who are without a voice and to be proactive in ultimately enabling them to speak for themselves. The Bible is replete with examples of God's care and compassion for His people, especially when they suffer; we see the vivid example of God leading the Israelites out of Egypt when they cried out to Him in their suffering. In Exodus 2: 23 -25, we read:

> The Israelites groaned in their slavery and cried out, and their cry for help because of their slavery went up to God. God heard and remembered their groaning and he remembered his covenant with Abraham, with Isaac and Jacob. So God looked on the Israelites and was concerned about them (NIV 1986).

Furthermore, Exodus 4:31 records that when the people hear of God's concern for them, it leads to belief and worship. As verse 31 says:

> So the people believed; and when they heard the Lord was concerned…and seen their affliction, then they bowed and worshipped (NIV 1986).

---

[13] John Corrie (ed.), [Cons. Eds]. J. Samuel Escobar, W.R. Shenk, *Dictionary of Mission Theology: Evangelical Foundation,* England: IVP 2007, 125.

I am convinced that this can happen for oppressed women as well; when they hear of God's compassion for them, in their oppression, it can lead to belief and worship.

I recently had correspondence from a friend who is in mission with her husband. They are involved in translating Scripture as well as working on programmes for oppressed women and children. She mentions how the women she meets live in such difficult circumstances, where wives are treated as servants, doing all the housework, beaten, seen only as child bearers, having to prove their fertility before marriage, the list goes on. Much is yet to be done for and by women.

But some feminists have always argued that women's issues are not only women's issues, they are also men's issues. Recently, in Ireland, a new alliance and campaign, under the banner *The Other Half*,[14] was launched by a men's group. This alliance works towards ending violence against women. They believe that the work to end violence against women can only be fully tackled by harnessing the energy, support and understanding of the additional 50 per cent of the population, that is, the men. The new alliance says:

> Men make up half the population. However, for a variety of reasons, violence against women has been largely tackled by women and has, by default, been seen as a women's issue. It is time to move on from this and to recognise men as potentially powerful allies in the fight against gender-based violence.

This is an example of a challenge from a secular organisation to the notion that women's issues are for women only and should be handled only by women. As Christians, we should be tackling the injustices against women with the full support and commitment of men and not just leaving it to women to lobby for change. Men also must be proactive with women in creating an environment where women are given full opportunity to use their gifts to serve the Lord and to live with dignity in a just society. In the history of India, some men have been actively engaged in working towards and securing women's rights, providing education and working

---

[14] The Other Half Campaign, *www.theotherhalf.ie*. R.T.E. *5/7 Live* Radio Programme, September 2010.

for the rights of children. For example, in the nineteenth century, Bengali Christian men, who were reformers, such as Rev. Krishna Mohan Banerjee and Rev. Bipin Chandra Sarkar, who worked with the Serampore Missionaries, Carey, Marshman and Ward.[15] The tireless work by men such as these changed society and history and the lives of so many. It is important also to remember the pioneering work of Hannah Marshman, known as the first woman Missionary,[16] to provide education for girls as well as boys. She laboured side by side with her husband Joshua. It is essential as believers that men and women engage together to enable women and indeed men to live with dignity. Pandita Ramabai is another example of an extraordinary, pioneering woman working for women's emancipation during this same period.[17]

Sadly, still today, women find themselves in some harrowing situations, in spite of so-called progress and technology. The evidence of poverty in women's lives and their ongoing abuse in sex trafficking is deeply distressing and has to be addressed. The sex tourism industry is an appalling evil and one of the tragic outcomes of globalisation. I cannot agree with those who suggest that any aspect of prostitution is a "lifestyle choice." This barbaric treatment of vulnerable women and children is unacceptable. We must continue to raise our voice against such wicked practices. Christians must be vigilantly outspoken on these issues, as much remains to be done. I am convinced this wickedness grieves the Lord greatly. As Christians, we have the unique opportunity to offer hope and redemption to women and children caught in such situations.

We celebrate and give thanks for such programmes; for example, as the "Women's Empowerment Programme" established by ISPCK, an initiative that challenges the mindset that keeps women in subjugation

---

[15] Dipankar Haldar, Select Bengali Christians as Reformers in the Pattern of Serampore Missionaries in *The Versatile William Carey*, W/Bengal, India: Serampore College, 2008, 50-53.

[16] Sunil Kumar Chatterjee, *Hannah Marshman: The First Woman Missionary in India*. Hoogly: Chatterjee 2006.

[17] D. Arthur Jeyakumar, *History of Christianity in India*, Delhi: ISPCK 2009.

and gives women opportunities to take control of their lives and live with dignity, and ultimately walk with their Saviour, Jesus Christ.

Jim Wallis in his book *Seven Ways to Change the World* mentions how he was recently reminded of the nineteenth-century heritage that we can look back to as Christians, following the great revivals, when the Anti-slave Trade Campaign was launched and Evangelical Christians, both men and women, were at the forefront of this great movement. He argues that the nineteenth-century mindset of calling for social justice by people of faith is now in the twenty-first century. By recalling this history, he fearlessly attempts to awaken the Western church from its reverie. He says:

> I strongly believe that faith matters and can make a difference, not only in our personal lives but in our world. The church's historians tell us that spiritual activity cannot be called revival until it has changed something in society...I believe the time is ripe for the kind of spiritual revival that leads to clear social commitments and outcomes. Revival is necessary because... getting to the right issues isn't enough...having the right message isn't enough...but people acting out of their deepest wells of faith can be an even more powerful thing...[18]

As a westerner recently visiting India, I have been blessed to see and hear of the amazing things that God is doing in India. In the West, we are experiencing the cynicism of a post-feminist and post-Christian society. Yet we long to see God do a great work of revival again, and we are thankful for what He is doing. We long for a fresh outpouring of His Spirit. We live in the hope that when God calls us to a task, whether we are in the East or the West, He is able to equip us and enable us to do it. God has given His gifts to the church, without a gender bias, without a bias of race or location. God's gifts are given graciously to both men and women for the good of the church body, to impact society around us and for His glory. Our responsibility is to heed and answer that call:

---

[18] Jim Wallis, *Seven Ways to Change the World: Reviving Faith and Politics*, Oxford: Lion, 2008, 251.

It is the Lord's prerogative to bestow gifts necessary for mission and to call those he so gifts to serve him in mission. It is our responsibility, whether we are women or men, to obey that call when it comes to us.[19]

May we each be sensitive and obedient to that call in our lives and faithfully serve our Saviour.

---

[19] Norman Shields, *Into all the World: What the Bible Teaches about Mission,* Wales: Bryntirion Press, 1998, 160.

Chapter 10

# Mission Engagement with Entertainment

## Place of Christian Story in Fiction and Film

### Davis Bunn

The objective of this talk is to examine the possible role that story might play within evangelical efforts in India. Two questions that must be addressed at the outset are, Can my experiences as a western writer of Christian fiction translate into something that is applicable to you in India? And second, Can novels and films be used for spreading the Gospel message in your culture and at this time?

This is a vital issue, and to understand it fully, it must be broken down into three components. The first is, Can Christian fiction and film be used for spreading the Gospel in any culture? The second is, Does inspirational fiction have any role to play in India? And finally, Can our experiences in building a successful American publishing industry for Christian fiction and a newly emerging market for Christian film be repeated here and now?

Cultural anthropologists have long claimed that every human society, no matter how far back in time, has told stories. Stories have been used as a means of instructing the young, of drawing the clan together and of holding fast to shared experiences and for the simple pleasure of being entertained. This is a vital and incontrovertible truth. Around the world, and throughout time, mankind has always told stories. Stories bind us together. They unite and strengthen and clarify. Story defines us as a people.

Good stories follow a very clear pattern, one that transcends both culture and distance. A reader wants a beginning, a middle and an end. The glory of Christ's message is how the concept of an ending is transformed. Beyond the story of Jesus lies yet another story. And this second story, the eternal significance, is one we cannot fully fathom, and yet one that we yearn for. We see now through a glass darkly, yet one day soon we will know and understand. It is finished, our Lord said, and yet the power of his story is that in truth, for us, it has only begun.

C. S. Lewis referred to inspirational fiction as, "Imagination in the service of truth." For Christian fiction to have any valid role at all, it must bring the reader closer to the eternal. For myself, the greatest joy in writing inspirational fiction is how, for some readers, the story does not end when the book is set down. Instead, some component of my story's message is woven into the fabric of their lives. The story lives in them. It challenges, or heals, or invites, or inspires. This to me is the only valid definition of inspirational fiction.

Fiction with an inspirational message becomes a base through which life is re-interpreted. The power of the words and the message they convey resonate at a level far beyond that of mere enjoyment or momentary pleasure. They transport the reader to a different perspective on life. This is a very important issue. The power of a good story lies in its ability to re-order lives.

This brings us to the issue of whether the concepts of Christian fiction and film have a role to play in India. Another way to frame this vital question would be, Is inspirational fiction a commercial concept in your country?

The word 'commercial' is an essential concept for us. This is especially true here and now. Unfortunately, Christian culture too often dismisses commercialism as directly at odds with the Gospel's message. We doubt the sincerity of those who come draped in the banner of success. And yet the only way our hosts, the highly venerated publisher ISPCK, can publish works and spread the Gospel next year is if they make money this year. The issue of commercial success is inescapable.

So in order to determine if my western experiences can possibly be translated to the Indian subcontinent, to help us see if inspirational fiction can indeed find success in this culture, I would like to share with you four fundamental lessons I have learned in my twenty-one years as a published author of inspirational fiction.

## Lesson One: *There are two kinds of readers in this world and seldom do they meet*

Around the world, classes in drawing and painting begin by offering the students a choice. The first lesson goes something like this: Throughout history, there have only been two ways of confronting the empty canvas; either the artist views the world as a flower, or as a geometric design. Everything else will flow from this one choice.

The same is true for writing. Either one approaches the empty page with the intention of designing a message, which orients one towards non-fiction, or one is first and foremost concerned with telling a story.

What is less recognised is how this dichotomy also exists within readers. The adage about readers goes like this: A reader who gravitates towards non-fiction reads to engage with the world. A reader who gravitates towards fiction reads to escape.

A fundamental problem in judging the commercial use of fiction in spreading the Gospel begins here. Why? Because most Christian leaders are oriented towards non-fiction. They read to learn. They remain students of the Gospel their entire lives.

But there is something more at work here. Too often, these same leaders view fiction as a distraction. Novels and film are part of the culture that opposes their work. They do not care for it and so they seek to disengage their work from the very concept of commercial fiction.

It is one thing to tell a story from the pulpit, and it is another thing entirely to invest time and money in the publishing of stories. This precept sadly dominates many Christian publishing houses, where the people in charge come from leadership positions in churches and do not hold a personal interest in fiction.

Until the late sixties, most major US publishers released the occasional story with a Christian moral. In fact, the top-selling hundred novels of the past century contained a number of Christian stories, including "The Robe", "Quo Vadis", "Christy", and "To Kill a Mockingbird." But gradually postmodernism came to dominate the publishing mindset, and by the mid-seventies the powers controlling New York publishing declared that God was dead.

In the late seventies, a manuscript arrived at Bethany House Publishers, which at the time only published Bible studies and Sunday School tracts. The novel told the story of a pioneer family facing ruin, and was written by a woman whose family had actually experienced such a trial. The Bethany House publishing board was dominated by pastors and theologians; they turned the book down. But the librarian at the school attached to the publishing house read the story and went before the board. She said that the book had the potential to sell ten thousand copies, an unheard-of amount at that time. The board refused to listen, but this librarian refused to back down. Reluctantly, after much argument, the board agreed. The book was entitled "Love Comes Softly", by Janette Oke. It went on to sell over three million copies and launched inspirational fiction in the United States. All because of one librarian, a lover of fiction, who forced a crowd of scholars and church leaders to change their mindset.

I wonder if the same potential for new and transformative success is waiting for you here in India, if someone has the courage and the foresight to change.

***Lesson Two: The cadence and structure of story changes with the medium***
This is a simple concept, but one with far-reaching consequences. Too often a teacher who can successfully tell a story at the pulpit assumes he

can also tell one on the page. Not only is this assumption incorrect, but their success at the pulpit can be a detriment to their writing.

Successful teachers often forget how long and hard they struggled to develop a style that draws people in, granting power to their lessons. Gradually, these tools become so ingrained as to be an almost unconscious extension of their teaching method. And these tools do not translate to the page. A good story from the pulpit may hold the potential for becoming a good story in written form. But it is only that— a potential.

The measure of a successful story can be reduced to this one adage: In a good book or film, the reader prefers the story's reality to their own. The structuring of such a good novel, where a multitude of readers set aside their cares and outside world to delve into your creation, is based upon the use of certain tools. These creative tools include the following: Seamless story arc, three dimensional characters, solid point of view, individuality in dialogue, separation of character motives and sub-plots that heighten story tension. Learning these lessons and applying these tools require time and dedication. I wrote for nine years and completed seven full-length novels before my first was accepted for publication. Most successful novelists and screenwriters have a similar learning curve to my own.

This is an indication of the level of commitment required to fashion good stories.

## *Lesson Three: Good stories require a professional perspective*

In the west, some Christian organisations foster an attitude that questions professionalism. Instead, amateurism is seen as preferable to commercial polish. If there is to be a successful and commercial application of story to spreading the Gospel, this must change.

This is true both in film and in fiction. Success in either requires an investment of capital and manpower. In order to move forward, two things must happen. First, there must be a commitment to the new direction. And second, there must be a system by which professional creativity is fostered at the grass-roots level.

My own personal dream would be to return here in five years' time and find a new arm to ISPCK that promotes novels and authors who have sprung from within the Indian culture. I would also dream of seeing films made in India that reveal the Gospel's eternal truths in stories that compete quality-wise with the best coming out of Bollywood.

This is also the standard I hold for myself personally. I seek to compete with the best of fiction that is being promoted by mainstream publishers and yet hold to our Lord's eternal truths. This to me is the essential challenge. So long as we hold to an attitude of amateurism, we reach only the converted. If we want to climb out of our self-imposed ghetto, if our aim is to reach the wider audience, we must accept the challenge of competition. We must deliver stories that the broader audience are hungry for. We must be professionals and present our work in a commercially successful fashion.

## *Lesson Four: A successful story contains just one moral or message*

Of all the concepts that prove hard for a successful pastor to understand, this is the toughest. And none are more essential to successful story telling. It is also why so many of the films made about the life of Jesus fall flat. They try to tell everything. And no matter how glorious the overall content may be, from a message standpoint, as a commercial story they fail.

It is also one reason why Mel Gibson's film "The Passion" succeeded so well. No matter what your personal impressions may be, it is important to remember that the movie made over half a billion dollars and was among the top ten films for the entire year in markets as diverse as Malaysia, Australia, South Africa, Brazil, Canada and all of Eastern Europe. Gibson limited his story to one essential message and time-frame: How earthly failure led to the gift of eternal life. When the actor playing Jesus uttered those telling words, "It is finished", a world-wide audience understood that it was, in truth, only the beginning.

But why is it necessary to limit the story to one lone message? Put simply, because a good story must reveal. If it is necessary to preach your message in order to get it across, you the author have failed as a story teller. The author's goal must be to create a structure whereby the reader discovers the message alongside the characters in the book. And besides this, the best messages also perform another critical function: They must be crucial to the story's climax.

If the main character realises the goal and comes to live the moral, then the story ends in triumph. If the main character chooses to turn away, the story becomes both a tragedy and a moral tale. Some of the most powerful stories in history are those where the main character fails and yet succeeds. We need look no further than Samson to understand the power of a lesson not learned.

The triumph of a good story permits different characters to reveal various aspects of the same message. There is an opportunity for the reader to gain a three-dimensional perspective on the moral and to see it live out in the lives of those who populate the page.

Having more than one moral or message bogs down the story. It is sadly an ingrained habit for many teachers, however. But more than one moral result simply dissolves the tension. It is no longer possible to reveal. Nor can the writer build up the tension, will the character learn this lesson or not. And the idea that their very life may depend upon gaining this one issue is lost. It is here that good stories begin to shift away from real life, in that every character and every segment of the plot must return to this moral dilemma. And perhaps this is why so many teachers find it difficult to accept this crucial edict. Life does not work this way. But we are not talking about life here. Remember what I said at the beginning. Our goal is to create a structure through which a new perspective on life is revealed. And to create a story with this sort of emotional power—one that can genuinely cause viewers to look at life anew—you must restrict your message to just one concept.

### *We live in an entertainment-driven world*

Current levels of revenue for new Bollywood releases, as well as rising trends for Indian television viewers, suggest this is as true for India as it is for the west. And the factor that ties all of these various components together, from books to electronic games, cinema and television, is the public's constant voracious hunger for new stories.

The issue that I cannot address, the critical question that only you can answer, is whether the Christian church in India today has any role to play in this rising demand for stories.

I would suggest that this issue is a component of a much larger issue, which is, where is your future outreach aimed?

If I understand this correctly, you as church leaders currently focus most of your efforts on the lower strata of Indian society. Your books, your preaching concepts and the themes that dominate your outreach programmes are by necessity fitted around this level of your culture. This to me suggests two questions.

First, are the members of your congregations and the people you intend to reach part of this rising surge in entertainment? If so, then it would suggest that you face both an opportunity and a risk. The opportunity is to tap into their love of entertainment and supply them with stories that both feed this hunger and inspire. But if you ignore this trend, you risk being sidelined, being seen as having no place within this vital component of their lives.

The second question is: Do you wish to grow beyond your current outreach and evangelical directions and touch the Indian society at large? I have heard enough about the problems you face to understand that this is a very touchy subject, with some very real risks. Even so, recognising the role story plays in their lives is vital. Who knows, perhaps a series of stories may be developed that introduce Christian moral concepts, without confronting your audience with the name of Jesus. There are Christian writers working in Hollywood, these days a place that is genuinely opposed to Christian values, whose goal is not, as they put it, to plant people in the pews. Instead, their aim is to reveal the Christian moral to an audience who otherwise would have no connection to our eternal hope. This must be done in very careful increments and couched in ways that do not invite hostility from our opponents. As a result of this approach, the number of Christians who work within the film and television community is currently growing at an exponential rate.

The issue I repeatedly hear about is how India's middle class is not just growing, but becoming a dominant force. If you as evangelists seek to involve yourselves in the lives of this thriving component of Indian society, it will be necessary to engage with them on their level, with a clear eye to their interests. In my opinion, story may provide the perfect conduit.

I wish you every possible success in all your vital ministries.

Chapter 11

# Preaching Christ in a Postmodern Culture

## From Congregations to Audiences

### Kieran Beville

> For the time is coming when people will not endure sound teaching, but having itching ears they will accumulate for themselves teachers to suit their own passions, and will turn away from listening to the truth and wander off into myths.
>
> 2 Timothy 4: 3[1]

In some sections of contemporary church, therapeutic rather than theological messages are sought and self-esteem is being cultivated instead of self-examination in the light of Scripture. People seem to want sound bites rather than sermons. Interestingly, Scripture identifies all sorts of ungodliness and irreligious attitudes, such as adultery, perversion, slave trading, lying and perjury, as contrary to sound doctrine. (1 Tim. 1:10). In view of this, it is important to uphold preaching as a means of conveying truth. I believe it is not only possible but also vitally necessary to preach Christ in contemporary culture.

---

[1] Unless otherwise stated all Scripture quotations are from the English Standard Version and used with permission.

Education was once a means of instilling virtue, training character and upholding the values of citizenship. Now, however, it has capitulated to the individualism and relativism of postmodern culture. Curricula have been debased by including misguided and experimental programmes in place of the tried and tested, true and trusted. The Christian church seems to be undergoing a similar process.

In some churches today, there is a tension between those who see themselves as the *avant-garde* and those who function as the rearguard. Some people regard churches as elitist institutions (like museums) that function as custodians of tradition. The following analogy may help to illustrate and examine a modern trend that has parallels in the evangelical church today.

Art galleries were once frequented to admire acclaimed works of great art exhibited for our education and aesthetic stimulation. Today, however, as a result of a desire to be more relevant and popular, by appealing to the masses, many of these galleries have become servants to novelty. They have forsaken what they deemed to be elitist in the belief that the space created would allow for the development of greater artistic vitality in their exhibitions. What has actually filled that vacuum is installation 'art' sometimes less aesthetic than a municipal landfill site!

## Vox Pop and Vanishing Pulpits

Is the church influenced by the market-driven economy in which we live, where packaging may even take priority over the product? Is the substance of the excellent and efficacious message of the gospel becoming subordinate? What was once a place of pulpits and pews is becoming a place of soapboxes and sofas, where puppeteers are preferred to preachers! The form in which truth is conveyed is important. 'Sermons' are beginning to sound more and more like pithy T-shirt slogans.

## Medium and Message

Many churches have moved towards a different way of conducting business that does not involve preaching. This is a reflection of what is happening in society where the nature of discourse has changed. In education, for example, the line between learner and teacher is becoming increasingly blurred. The egalitarian spirit that pervades education invites us to 'explore' issues rather than have them 'explained.' This indicates a significant shift in our thinking.

The preacher is under pressure to keep everything brief and not overtax the attention but to provide constant stimulation through variety and novelty. Bite sized messages are favoured and complexity must be avoided. Ultimately, this produces emotionally stimulated but biblically illiterate congregations. Preaching is meant to be transformative, not inert. It is not merely about imparting information. There has to be an information-action ratio where relevant information is generated into action.

In the commercial world, there is a difference between *product* research and *market* research. The balance has shifted in favour of market research and the church seems to have followed this pattern. Instead of making sermons of value, some are engaged in making the congregation (consumers) feel valuable. Preaching has, therefore, become pseudo-psychotherapy in the overall drama of the service. The psychological need of the hearers is paramount rather than the Word of God.

Enjoyment is taken, first, as a means to an end and then as an end in itself. So we are led to expect to be emotionally stimulated and reject anything that does not deliver this. Systematic teaching, however, lays a foundation and this takes time and commitment on both the parts of the preacher and the hearer. It also assumes that the *growth* of the hearer is paramount. But where the *contentment* of the hearer is of greater importance the message must be pleasing. There is a pressure to increase stimulation at the expense of education and in the absence of exposition, entertainment is the result.

## Charming the Church

Preaching is the missing note in the music of mission today. Some churches have become engaged in experiments to accommodate themselves to the market-driven expectations of the world. The principle seems to be that if you want to get your share of the audience, you must offer them something they want. The church can be popular if it is prepared to trivialise preaching, and some think that is a price worth paying. This process begins when a church desires to be more acceptable and pleasing to the community. This may be a good desire but it can become an unhealthy obsession leading to compromising changes. At first, changes made by a church in its practice may seem benign. Is the church being mesmerised by entertainment values?

I grew up in Limerick City in Ireland where the river Shannon was a dominant feature of the geographical landscape as well as the recreational and occupational life of the people. My maternal grandfather and uncles were fishermen who earned a living from this river. In my lifetime, that great waterway has been slowly polluted and it is no longer suitable for bathing. It is amazing what can be lost in a generation.

The church is like a river insofar as changes in its life are sometimes gradual and imperceptible at first. Like the river it can be slowly polluted. It takes time before it becomes so poisonous that the fish die. Yet the river looks the same as before and one could still take a boat ride on it. In other words, even when life has been taken from it, the river does not disappear, nor do all of its uses but its value has been diminished and its degraded condition will have harmful effects throughout the landscape.

Boating is now a leisure activity on the Shannon but in a previous generation, life was sustained by the fish caught in that great waterway. The river is still there but it is not what it used to be and it is not what it appears to be. So it is with the church that is being slowly polluted. If a church merely has a recreational function in the life of the community, it has ceased to be what it ought to be.

It no longer seems strange now for some to have church events where there is no preaching; for example, what is sometimes called, 'low-key evangelism.' Various activities can be arranged in the church building with the purpose in mind to 'just get people across the threshold' and into a 'non-threatening environment.' This has come to seem natural and is an indication of a desire to be inoffensive. But the desire to be accepted and the need to appear relevant may turn the church in the wrong direction.

If the business of the church is preaching the Word of God, then some churches are facing bankruptcy. The demise of preaching is part of a wider issue, namely the crisis of confidence in biblical wisdom, its sufficiency and efficacy. But preaching is a conduit for the power of God in mission.

## Preaching Christ in a Postmodern Culture

The psalmist asks, "If the foundations are destroyed, what can the righteous do?" (Ps. 11:3). We live in a society where the very concept of objective, absolute truth is perceived not just as antiquated but absurd. The search for an apologetic strategy in postmodern society is a formidable challenge for the Christian church. Is the apologetic task feasible in a culture that denies the existence of objective, universal truth?

Under the auspices of modernity, colonialism and capitalism flourished, fascism threatened to destroy Europe and was countered by Marxist social experiments, which quarantined millions from what it perceived as the evils of free market economics. In short, modernity failed to create the utopia to which it aspired and these conflicting ideologies came to be seen as, 'totalising oppressive meta-narratives.' In postmodernity, Christianity too has come to be viewed as a discredited meta-narrative.

There has been a significant shift in thinking, which has relevance to those engaged in preaching. In the modernist mindset, if something could be proved as true, or at least reasonable, the logical conclusion was that it ought to be accepted. Whereas the modernist who accepted the veracity of the Christian message was being hypocritical in not accepting its personal implications, the postmodernist is not constrained in this way.

In any sermon, there is a particular line of thought where judgements and application are made in a coherent and orderly arrangement of argument. Preaching, therefore, assumes a competence in its hearers where the objective use of the mind is taken for granted. It is not that it is essentially intellectual but that it is inherently rational. In other words, it assumes that reason is employed to enlighten. People may be moved emotionally by preaching but they are required firstly to understand its content.

Preaching is, after all, expositing a text that has syntactical structure and content that can be explicated. There is, therefore, not just a faith in the truth of the text but also faith in reason itself. It engages the intellect and passions as well as the soul and will. It assumes that people are rational and analytical creatures. It is essentially a serious undertaking that conveys biblical information and makes claims in propositional form.

A sermon, of course, does not, necessarily, guarantee true content, for preachers are flawed and frail. However, it does, at least, construct a context in which the question 'Is this true or false?' is relevant and meaningful. Whether it is sophisticated or simple, it appeals to cognitive powers based on understanding and reason. As traditionally understood, preaching has a bias towards the ability to think conceptually, deductively and sequentially and because it is based on reason and order it has an inherent aversion for contradiction.

Preaching, we know, is not merely about knowing facts, even biblical facts; it involves an understanding of the implications, historical background and logical and theological connections. But in the postmodern world, reality has been dismembered, meanings have been wrenched out of logical contexts and life has become idiosyncratic. The postmodern mindset has a predisposed antipathy to preaching because it is influenced by the philosophy of the age. Logic, reason, sequential thought and rules of contradiction are abandoned.

Thus it does not seem to matter that some 'truths' in the postmodern world actually contradict each other. How can this be explained? Contradiction requires mutually exclusive assertions that cannot possibly both, in the same context, be true. It is context, therefore, that defines contradiction. If somebody says he prefers grapes to peaches and then also says that he prefers peaches to grapes, there is not, necessarily, a contradiction if one statement is made in the context of choosing a pattern for curtains and the other expresses his eating preference. But if these statements are made in a singular context, say, in relation to decor alone, they are contradictory. Without a continuous and coherent context there is no such thing as contradiction.

Therefore, when preaching the gospel is taken out of the context of linear history and presented in a world of discontinuity and fragmentation, it is 'a truth' that does not contradict 'other truths.' The Bible, for example, presents us with a certain degree of Palestinian history. It has one continuous and coherent perspective. In today's world, it is just one version of truth where contradictory perspectives have equal validity because culture is seen as the defining context.

To what extent, therefore, if any, should the message or methodology be modified to adapt to a world that is postmodern? How can an apologetic strategy be shaped that is relevant in the context of postmodernity and uncompromising in its eternal message?

Individualism and relativism are features of our society. It is not unlike the situation that prevailed in Israel at the time of the Judges, before the authority of the king emerged, "In those days there was no king in Israel. Everyone did what was right in his own eyes" (Judges 21:25). If individualism and relativism are features of our culture, then there is a great need for the church to counter this by modelling transformed communities. In a society where rational discourse has failed, we ought to manifest the reality of the power of God in radically altered lives.

We should take heed to the warning of Paul to the Galatian Church: "See to it that no one takes you captive by philosophy and empty deceit, according to human tradition, according to the elemental spirits of the world, and not according to Christ" (Col. 2:8).

Increasingly, we find that churches are being influenced by postmodernity. Some evangelical churches are becoming theologically foggy and non-doctrinal. In such churches, there is an appeal to feelings that puts emotionalism at the centre of practice and this in turn affects preaching. We are beginning to see a shift of emphasis from truth to technique. In this market-driven and consumer-oriented culture, psychology tends to eclipse Christology. Postmodernity trivialises the transcendent truth of the gospel.

The desire to be relevant must be subordinate to the obligation to be faithful. Where the desire to be relevant is uppermost unpalatable truths may be sidelined as 'unhelpful.' In such circumstances, there is an admission that these truths are unmarketable. Although all communication is based on common ground, it must be acknowledged that Christians have a message to proclaim, which runs counter to the prevailing world-view.

To silently model Christlikeness and ignore preaching would be a contradiction because Christ engaged in proclamation. We cannot dismiss the Word of God as irrelevant in a postmodern society because God says that his Word will never be void of power (Isa. 55:10-11). His Word must be wielded in preaching as a spiritual weapon because it is "sharper than any two-edged sword, piercing to the division of soul and of spirit" (Heb. 4:12).

Paul's instruction to Timothy applies to us, "preach the word; be ready in season and out of season; reprove, rebuke, and exhort, with complete patience and teaching" (2 Tim. 4:2). Yet it is important that we are informed about the mindset of people today. It is interesting to note that on the list of people who came to join David in battle at a crucial juncture in the history of Israel, there were "men who had understanding of the times, to know what Israel ought to do" (1 Chron. 12:32). We need such people today at an equally crucial juncture in the history of God's people.

Jesus said, "I am the way, and the truth, and the life. No one comes to the Father except through me" (John 14:6). Peter and John proclaimed: "There is salvation in no one else, for there is no other name under heaven given among men by which we must be saved" (Acts 4:12). These words are no more and no less politically correct than they were in the first century. They may engender the same kind of hostility today as they did then. In seeking to find an apologetic strategy that is contemporary, we must be unapologetic about preaching Christ, "we preach Christ crucified, a stumbling block to Jews and folly to Gentiles" (1 Cor. 1:23). To the world, our preaching may be merely discredited rhetoric: "For the word of the cross is folly to those who are perishing, but to us who are being saved it is the power of God" (1 Cor. 1:18).

But how we live in our culture is also crucial. Daniel, for example, found himself in Babylon. He made a conscious decision that he would not be overwhelmed by the culture of his day. But Scripture recounts how, "Daniel resolved that he would not defile himself with the king's food" (Dan. 1:8). In this he is exemplary.

When John the Baptist was imprisoned and began to doubt that Jesus was the Messiah, he sent messengers to Jesus to inquire if he was really the Christ. It is very interesting to see how Jesus replied: "Go and tell John what you have seen and heard: the blind receive their sight, the lame walk, lepers are cleansed, and the deaf hear, the dead are raised up, the poor have good news preached to them" (Luke 7:22).

John doubted the deity of Jesus and doubted all that he had preached in heralding the Christ. Jesus does not give a theological dissertation on the fulfilment of prophecy in the person and work of Christ. No, he asks the messengers to report what they have witnessed of the transforming power of God as demonstrated in his miracles. His activity authenticated his authority. To those who doubt and despair, we must be messengers from the Saviour who talk as first-hand witnesses of the transforming power of Christ—"That...which we have heard, which we have seen with our eyes, which we looked upon and have touched with our hands, concerning the word of life" (1 John 1:1). This is important in a postmodern culture where winning arguments is not so much impossible as irrelevant. The gospel is not just about words of persuasion but also about pointing to evidence of that transforming power and *being* evidence of that power. Christians have a transforming vision to transmit but not just with words. When reason and rational argument fail, relationship might fill the vacuum.

## Preaching that Persuades

The notion of persuasion in postmodern culture has to be reconceived. It is not to be equated with the modernist notion where it is essentially about being intellectually convinced of the truth of an argument. It should, rather, be understood in classical terms. Ancient Greek and Roman civilisation was devoted to the dynamics of public-speaking. Plato, Aristotle, Cicero and others contributed to the development of the rhetorical art form. Aristotle's seminal work, *Rhetoric*, was the standard text for the times. Aristotle categorised the rhetorical art of persuasion in three divisions. Firstly, he deals with *ethos*, which focuses on the integrity of the speaker. Secondly, he deals with *logos*, which is about the inherent logic of the message itself. Thirdly, he deals with *pathos*, which is about the emotions evoked by the oration.

The integrity of the preacher, the authority of the Word and the appeal to emotions are all relevant factors in preaching. In modernism, the stress was on the authority of the Word (*logos*) above the others (*ethos* and *pathos*). But in postmodernism, there is an emphasis on emotions, where truth is seen as a matter of individual belief and morality is governed by the principle, 'if it feels good, it is good.' The importance of the preacher's integrity cannot be underestimated. His moral character may influence how the message itself is perceived. Augustine said, 'The life of the speaker has greater weight in determining whether he is obediently heard than any grandness of eloquence.'[2]

Certainly a lack of integrity undermines credibility. There is a connection between preaching and practice insofar as the moral stature of the messenger contributes to enhancing the reception of the message. Effectiveness in preaching is not ultimately determined by the eloquence of the preacher, the soundness of his logic, the virtue of the man or indeed all of these factors combined. George Whitfield's biographer comments:

> Whitfield's...effectiveness lay not in his eloquence or zeal. As we look back from our present standpoint we see that God's chosen time to 'arise and have mercy upon Zion...yea, the set time had come,' and that in raising up Whitfield, He had granted upon him and his ministry 'a mighty effusion of the Holy Ghost': and it was this, the Divine power, which was the first secret of his success.[3]

An examination of Paul's thinking and methods of communication shows that his success is never attributed to convincing people of the veracity of propositional truth claims. It was not enough for Paul to announce

---

[2] Augustine, Aurelius (Saint), *On Christian Doctrine*, 4.27.59.

[3] Dallimore, Arnold, *George Whitfield, The Life and Times of the Great Evangelist of the 18th Century Revival*, Banner of Truth Trust, 1980, vol. 1, 116-117.

the truth, either evangelistically, as revealed in the book of *Acts*, or pastorally as revealed in his epistles. Paul's preaching met with resistance too. Paul had to persuade people (even in the church) of the gospel and its implications (for example, Galatians). The key to understanding preaching is to realise that there is a difference between 'persuading' and 'pronouncing.' It is a difference in attitude and tone that is almost intuitively conveyed, but it is an important difference in a world where style takes precedence over substance.

Paul's approach to presenting the gospel involved *reasoning, explaining* and *proving* in an effort to see people persuaded. He used his intellectual faculties and theological training to demonstrate the truth of his message by drawing on evidence from Old Testament Scripture. The Bereans tested the accuracy of his claims by searching the Scriptures in order to establish the validity of his assertions. A number of them found that there was sufficient evidence to warrant a verdict of proven and yielded to its consequential demand for faith.

Paul sought to persuade people of the truth of the gospel. This is clear in Acts chapters 17-19 in particular. It is revealed that in Thessalonica, "Paul went in, as was his custom, and on three Sabbath days he reasoned with them from the Scriptures, explaining and proving that it was necessary for the Christ to suffer and to rise from the dead" (Acts 17:2-3).

Clearly Paul is engaged in expository preaching of the Old Testament in a reasonable, rational and persuasive manner. Then Paul travelled to Athens where he reasoned in the synagogue and in the marketplace (Acts 17:17). When in Corinth, Paul continued with the same approach, reasoning in the synagogue every Sabbath (Acts 18:4). Paul's enemies knew him to be a person who sought to persuade others to convert from Judaism to Christianity. They said, "This man is persuading people to worship God contrary to the law" (Acts 18:13). In Ephesus, Paul is found arguing persuasively (Acts 19:8). When Festus accused Paul of insanity, he replied that what he was saying was true and reasonable (Acts 26:25).

But Paul was conscious that it was not enticing words or eloquence that prevailed upon people to be receptive and responsive to the message.

He does not attribute their conversions to plausible argumentation. He attributes the 'success' of his preaching to the operation of the power of the Holy Spirit in stirring the minds and emotions of his hearers to persuade them to yield their wills to the will of God.

Paul preached Christ with passion and power and sought to be as persuasive as possible in the manner in which he presented his message. His discourse was rational and coherent and characterised by a fervent desire to see people coming to faith in Christ. It is obvious that others (such as Agrippa) recognised this tone in his preaching (Acts 26:28). In his second letter to the Corinthians, Paul explicitly states that he intentionally set about seeking to persuade people of the truth of the gospel (5:11). When persuasion is used in connection with religious proclamation today, it is often associated with arrogance and intolerance. Fernando draws attention to how peculiar this is:

> This is strange because persuasion is used daily in many spheres of life. Advertisers seek to persuade us to patronize certain products, and politicians seek to persuade us to accept their policies and vote for them. Yet when it comes to religion, this approach to communication is considered inappropriate.[4]

Paul was aware that understanding the truth of the gospel is a matter of spiritual discernment. It is the Holy Spirit that enables the mind to apprehend truth and that intellectual comprehension stimulates impulses that determine decisions. In the words of Calvin, "The effectual cause of faith is not the perspicacity of our mind, but the calling of God." It is not, therefore, merely a mental matter. Paul was aware that coming to know divine truth was not the result of speculation but rather the result of revelation and illumination (1 Cor. 2:14). Nevertheless, he did what he could to make the message clear and intelligible. Again the book of Acts confirms this. Whether it was the synagogue or the marketplace, Paul laboured day after day to present the gospel in as persuasive a manner as possible. This was also his typical approach in Thessalonica and Ephesus.

---

[4] Ajith Fernando, 'The Uniqueness of Jesus Christ', 127.

In the postmodern climate, the rules of engagement have changed. Argumentation in Paul's day was based on the refined outcome of centuries of Greek thought. There was an established framework for determining truth claims. Rules of logic may not be perfect but to discard them altogether is absurd. D. A. Carson speaks of this revolt against absolutes:

> For the first time in the history of the church...the only heresy that's left is the view that there is such a thing as heresy - that is the one heretical view. And within this kind of framework to preach an unflinching truth, and to claim that apart from this truth men and women are eternally lost makes you not only sound 'nineteenth century' and bigoted, but irrelevant and hopelessly lost in an epistemology now dead just crying out for a decent burial.[5]

According to Scripture, God reasons with sinners (Isa. 1:18). If Paul is taken to be a superior model of effective communication to which Christian preachers should aspire, then his style must be scrutinised to see what principles may be extrapolated from such a model.

Passion is an important element of preaching. If preaching is seeking to convey information to the mind alone, then people may understand the meaning of the message but fall short of undertaking its demands. If a sermon is presented like a lecture or a dissertation on a theme, it may convince the intellect but not captivate the soul. Preaching to the soul engages the mind, emotions and will. Truth must be spoken to the mind with calculated intent to stir the emotions and engage the will. Preaching seeks to provoke a whole-soul response. The aim of preaching is not just to get people to comprehend the truth but to embrace it.

Wariness of the seductive charms of preachers is part of the cynicism of this generation. The Christian communicator is not marketing a product or trying to soft-soap, sugar-coat or sell to potential consumers. Persuasive preaching is not about trying to clinch deals.

## Humility

Humility should be the hallmark of a preacher, as it was an essential element in the ministry of Christ. But humility can be misplaced, as G. K. Chesterton observed:

---

[5] Carson, D. A., *The Primacy of Expository Preaching*, cassette.

> What we suffer from today is humility in the wrong place. Modesty has moved from the organ of ambition. Modesty has settled on the organ of conviction, where it was never meant to be. A man was meant to be doubtful about himself, but undoubting about the truth; this has been exactly reversed. We are on the road to producing a race of men too mentally modest to believe in the multiplication table.[6]

The humility of the messenger is important but this does not mean humility regarding the message. The message of Scripture must be proclaimed with a confidence appropriate to its importance

I believe that preaching Christ is still feasible in postmodern culture. It is important that the church understands the historical and philosophical development of postmodernism. We must recognise that the Enlightenment project is deemed to have failed and Christianity is perceived as an oppressive meta-narrative. In a world that is becoming increasingly sceptical and where preaching practitioners are becoming disillusioned, some guidelines about preaching to postmoderns are needed. In a relational age, rationality is impotent and so the notion of persuasion needs to be redefined as a whole-soul influence affecting the mind, emotions and the will. Understanding the difference between authoritative and authoritarian preaching allows hope for the survival of the homiletic task. We need signposts for a way forward in the labyrinthine complexity of the new paradigm. This is a challenge to all those engaged in the homiletic task. Christian leaders need to understand the powerful wind shift of postmodernism and the ways it is affecting society. Preachers must reset their sails to become effective. The importance of addressing this issue in homiletic training cannot be overstated. We need to provide clear and useful insights for understanding the elusive nature of postmodernity. But let us not lose confidence in the power of Christ-centred, Spirit-filled preaching as an essential element in our mission strategy.

---

[6] Cited by Stewart, James S., *Heralds of God: A Practical Book on Preaching*, Regent College Publishing, 1946, 210.

# The Way Forward ...

Poised on the momentous occasion of the 300th Anniversary of the SPCK in India and

Deliberating on the Mission of ISPCK Beyond 2010.....

We pause at this historic moment in time to

*Celebrate* 300 years of Ministry through Christian literature in India,

*Acknowledge* the challenge and the struggle of ISPCK to be relevant and inspiring through the centuries that witnessed sweeping changes both within the country and across the world

*Affirm* the long and rewarding journey of Indianisation and diversification not only in the range, scale and scope of its Ministries, but also in the large contribution it has made to Indian churches and society.

*Appreciate* its efforts to synergize and blend its opportunities to change with time, situation and context and

*Commend* its compelling vision in promoting Christian thought and values, and a commitment that looks beyond the market forces.

We also pause at this significant moment to attempt to refashion the stated Mission objectives of ISPCK, to formulate a forward-looking Mission beyond 2010 that would seek to encompass within the ambit of its activities strategies that would deal with the rapidly changing face of the world in all its entirety... both imaginable and unimaginable.

While we reaffirm the basic Mission of ISPCK that propelled it through the centuries by:

- Communicating Christian faith in its rich diversity
- Helping people to understand it and develop their personal faith
- Equipping Christians for Mission and Ministry

We *recommend* that it would strive:

- To develop and articulate, from the emerging contextual theologies, an authentic Indian Public Theology that would focus on empowering the mission of the church to recognise her call and feed her peoples, both spiritually and physically.
- To articulate an inclusive biblical hermeneutics that emphasises the needs of the poor and the marginalised, especially the empowerment of women and children.

## The Way Ahead

We pray that ISPCK may therefore continue in the following:

**Enabling** role to explore opportunities for growth and partnership among churches, church leaders, academicians and lay people in their quest for spiritual growth

**Empowering** indigenous talent and the potentialities of women and children so that they are visible and can contribute meaningfully to the enrichment of Christian understanding

**Engaging** the energies and talents of all Christian denominations to complement each other rather than compete with each other, resulting in a better understanding of Mission

**Enriching all** sections of society by making available to people Christ-centred books that are relevant in the context of religious plurality

**Equipping** people to move beyond the parameters of tradition and culture to build bridges that would help to reach out to everybody in love and faith

**Educating** the marginalised and the suppressed by reaching out to them with resources that are liberating and encouraging

**Equipping** existing and new capabilities with tools and timely capacity building to bring out their creative best for the edification of society

**Exploring** alternative styles of communication that will be attractive and competent in a world of technological advances

**Encouraging** lifestyles that would defeat the adverse effects of consumerism and would seek to return to the simple and tested styles rooted in the wisdom and practices of our communities

**Emphasising** the need to neutralise crippling market forces by advocating for economic policies that support inclusive growth, sustain life and ensure equitable sharing of resources.

And to realise that there has to be a major paradigm shift from the single-ministry society of spreading good news to a multi-dimensional ministry that would bring home the truth that the only paradigm worth its salt is the paradigm of reconciliation in the midst of the emerging forces of convergence and forces of destruction, so that we celebrate unity and harmony within the rich diversity of this great nation... A unity that will heal and help in building communities of just peace.

## Submitted by

**Rev. Dr. Papiya Durairaj**
**Rev. Dr. Richard Rodgers**
**Rev. Dr. P. G. George**
**Dr. Mar Atsongchanger**
**Rev. Dr. Ipe Joseph**
**Prof. Dr. Leonard Fernando**
**Mrs. Susan Jacob**

# Contributors

**Prof. Dr. Felix Wilfred** from the Roman Catholic Church in Tamil Nadu is Founder-Director of Asian Centre for Cross-Cultural Studies, Chennai and the President of Concilium. He is Professor, Indian Council of Cultural Relations (ICCR), University of Dublin, Ireland. Earlier, he was the Chairperson of the School of Philosophy and Religious Thought and President of the Faculty of Arts, University of Madras. His previous works published by ISPCK include *On the Banks of Ganges, The Sting of Utopia, Asian Dreams and Christian Hope, Margins – The Site of Asian Theologies* and *Asian Public Theology: Critical Concerns in Challenging Times*. He currently serves as Editor, *Concilium*.

**Dr. Kieran Beville** is an experienced Christian newspaper columnist. A former teacher of English (language and literature), History, Communications and Media Studies, he is now Pastor of the Lee Valley Bible Church (Baptist) in Cork, Ireland. He had taught theology on leadership training programmes in Eastern Europe and Biblical Studies in India. He is an international conference speaker on the themes of Mission, Postmodernism and Preaching and has authored *Exploring Ezra: The Secret of Spiritual Success* (Day One Publications, 2004), *Cultivating Christian Character: The Fruit of the Spirit* (Day One Publications, 2005), *Jonah: Pride and Prejudice* (ISPCK, 2010) *and Preaching Christ in a Postmodern Culture* (Cambridge Scholars Publishing, 2010). E-mail: bevillekieran@gmail.com

# Contributors

**Dr. Monica Jyotsna Melanchthon** of the Lutheran Church in India teaches Old Testament at the Gurukul Lutheran Theological College, Chennai. She has explored into creative hermeneutical explorations as revealed in her writings: *Rejection by God: The History and Significance of the Rejection Motif in the Hebrew Bible* (Studies in Biblical Literature, Vol. 22); "A Fresh Look at Jesus Christ" (paper presented to NCC Assembly, 1996) and numerous other articles.

**Rev. Dr. Roger Gaikwad** is the General Secretary of NCCI, holds a Doctor of Theology degree in Religion from South Asia Theological Research Institute. He taught at Aizawl Theological College, Mizoram, and later served as its Principal. Also, he served as Chairman, Student Christian Movement of India. In addition, he served the Senate of Serampore College at SCEPTRE, Kolkata, and has been involved in leadership roles. He currently serves as General Secretary, National Council of Churches of India.

**Rev. Dr. Sunil M. Caleb** obtained his Ph.D. from the University of Canterbury. Currently, he serves as Principal, Bishop's College, Kolkata, West Bengal, where he also teaches Theology. E-mail: smcaleb@vsnl.net

**Prof. Dr. Siga Arles** obtained his early theological education from Asbury Theological Seminary, USA, and Ph.D. from the University of Aberdeen (Centre for Study of Christianity in the Non-Western World). He has authored *Missiological Education: An Indian Exploration,* Bangalore: CFCC, 2006. As Professor of Missiology, he taught at Serampore College, directed CIME, IIMRC, and currently directs publications and academic research studies at Centre for Contemporary Christianity, Bangalore. (#47, 10th Cross, 3rd Main, Hoysala Nagar, Ramamurthy Nagar Extn, Bangalore 560016, India. *arles@sify.com*)

**Rev. Dr. Richard Howell** of the Evangelical Church of India serves as General Secretary, Evangelical Fellowship of India. He has also served as Principal, Allahabad Bible Seminary, and is currently Secretary, Evangelical Fellowship of Asia. In addition, he has given leadership to the closer working together of EFI with NCCI and CBCI and has authored several articles and edited books on religious freedom and liberty. See *Free to Choose: Issues in Conversion, Freedom of Religion and Social Engagement,* Delhi: EFI, 2002.

**Bernadette O Connell Beville** along with her husband Kieran from Ireland was a resource person at the ISPCK Tercentenary Mission Consultation in Delhi, 2010.

**Dr. Davis Bunn** from the Unites States of America is a Christian writer of fictions and has explored into promoting Christian involvement in film and fiction for the sake of mission among the peoples who are not yet aware of the gospel of Jesus Christ.

# List of Participants

1. Mrs. Alila
2. Rev. Amrit Mundu
3. Rt. Rev. Anand Chandulal
4. Adv. Anjana Masih
5. Mr. Ankur V. Samuel
6. Ms. Asangla
7. Rev. Dr. Ashish Amos
8. Major Ashok
9. Mr. Atul Peter
10. Rt. Rev. Basil B. Baskey
11. Mrs. Ber Beville
12. Rev. Dr. Chilkuri Vasantha Rao
13. Mr. Davis Bunn
14. Mr. Deepak Acharya
15. Mr. Deepak Masih
16. Mrs. Ella Sonawane

17. Rt. Rev. Ernest W. Talibuddin
18. Rt. Rev. Ezra Sargunam
19. Prof. Dr. Felix Wilfred
20. Fr. Francis Gonsalves
21. Prof. George W. Surendra
22. Mr. Hepesh Shepherd
23. Mrs. Hrangthan Chhungi
24. Rev. Dr. Ipe Joseph
25. Dr. J. T. K. Daniel
26. Mrs. J.T.K. Daniel
27. Rev. James Gomez
28. Rev. Dr. Kieren Beville
29. Mr. Lal Wijesinghe
30. Prof. Dr. Leo Fernando
31. Ms. Lilymith Lepcha
32. Ms. Lucy Holt
33. Rev. Dr. Mar Atsongchanger
34. Dr. Monica Melanchthon
35. Dr. Moses Manohar
36. Dr. O. M. Rao
37. Rev. Dr. P. G. George
38. The Most Rev. P. P. Marandih
39. Dr. Dn. Papiya Durairaj
40. Rt. Rev. Paul Dupare

## List of Participants

41. Mrs. Praveena Balasundaram
42. Mr. Peter Gunasekaran
43. Mr. Rajesh Williams
44. Rev. Dr. Richard Howell
45. Rev. Dr. Richard Rodgers
46. Mrs. Rochelle
47. Rev. Dr. Roger Gaikwad
48. Rev. Samson Peters
49. Prof. Dr. Siga Arles
50. Mr. Simon Kingston
51. Ms. Sue Tennant
52. Mr. Sundeep Chawdhry
53. Rev. Dr. Sunil M. Caleb
54. Rt. Rev. Surya Prakash
55. Mrs. Susan Jacob
56. Mr. Thilal
57. Ms. Udeshika Costa
58. Mrs. Vidhupriya Chakravarty
59. Rev. Dr. Vincent Rajkumar
60. Dr. Vinodh Gunasekera

www.ingramcontent.com/pod-product-compliance
Lightning Source LLC
Chambersburg PA
CBHW031954080426
42735CB00007B/389